❦ *Memoirs of a Bookman*

Other Books by Jack Matthews

Novels

Sassafras

The Charisma Campaigns

Pictures of the Journey Back

The Tale of Asa Bean

Beyond the Bridge

Hanger Stout, Awake!

Short story Collections

Ghostly Populations

Crazy Women

Dubious Persuasions

Tales of the Ohio Land

Bitter Knowledge

Poems

An Almanac for Twilight

Non-fiction

Booking in the Heartland

Collecting Rare Books for Pleasure and Profit

Archetypal Themes in the Modern Story

The Writer's Signature: Idea in Story and Essay (edited with Elaine Hemley)

Memoirs of a Bookman

❦ Jack Matthews

OHIO UNIVERSITY PRESS ❦ *ATHENS*

Reprinted 1990
Library of Congress Cataloging-in-Publication Data
Matthews, Jack.
    Memoirs of a bookman / Jack Matthews.
        p.   cm.
    Includes bibliographical references.
    ISBN 0-8214-0937-9 (alk. paper)
        1. Matthews, Jack. 2. Antiquarian booksellers—United States—
Biography. 3. Rare books—Collectors and collecting. 4. Book
collecting—United States. 5. Rare books—Bibliography. I. Title.
Z473.M26   1990
381'.45002'092—dc20
[B]   89-37615
                                                                   CIP

Ohio University Press books are printed on acid-free paper ∞

ACKNOWLEDGMENTS

"Rare Book Dealing, or Solace in Blunderland" was read before
the Pittsburgh Bibliophiles, Pittsburgh, PA, May 19, 1988.

"Old Laughs" was read before the Conference on ALICE-type Systems
at Ohio University, on April 24, 1986.

"Perhaps the Greatest Incomparable Autobiography in the World"
was delivered at a meeting of NOBS (the Northern Ohio Bibliophilic Society)
on May 24, 1986, at Kent State University.

"Cockfights, Hound Dogs, and Preachers" was delivered at the
banquet of the Southeast Ohio Chapter Conference of the Ohio
Library Association, March 27, 1987, in Nelsonville, Ohio.

I would also like to thank Timeline *(of the Ohio Historical Society)*
and The Ohio Magazine, *in which other pieces from this collection
have been, or are scheduled to be, published.*

I would also like to express my gratitude to The Ohio Arts Council for being awarded a
Major Artist Award for 1989–90.

This book is dedicated to

the perpetuation of the printed word,

the instrumentality of the computer,

and the flourishing of trees.

❧ Contents

Rare Book Dealing, or Solace in Blunderland

The transition from collecting rare books to dealing in them is a natural, though not inevitable, progression. I know book collectors who have no temptation to deal in books, and I know dealers who appear to be totally immune to any of the virulent strains of collecting, even to those new strains that keep emerging just as nasty new strains of real, non-metaphorical viruses keep doing.

Those who collect rare books without any temptation to deal in them belong to a small and very exclusive class. They collect the first editions of one author, let us say, or one well-defined group of authors, or perhaps just one sort of book (i.e., pre-1920 novels featuring automobile travel or English color plate books from 1800 to 1840), but it all stops there. By "it," I mean their purchasing. If they collect the first editions of British mystery writers in the 1920's, these people won't even look at a Faulkner first edition. If they collect midwestern Americana, they can hardly bear to contemplate the existence of first editions of Wallace Stevens or Anthony Trollope.

Such people are often thought of as being among the blessed of this earth; they know what they want and they go about getting it. They are marvels of discipline. They appear to be so secure in knowing what they like, and so admirable in their self control, that I don't see how they can stand it. Individuals were not meant to contain so much prudence and self-knowledge. Self-knowledge is a Socratic ideal, and we know where ideals belong—somewhere up in the air, or in the future; anywhere but in our behavior. And as for prudence . . . well, a little goes a long way, and it certainly was never meant to take over a whole personality and dominate it the way it is said a neurotic person can sometimes dominate a family or perhaps even some larger social unit.

No doubt my sullen envy is manifest. I am deficient in character, and if I had more of it, I would be ashamed of the fact. The disgraceful, even disgusting, truth is, I do collect some of the books in those categories mentioned above, and with only the slightest nudge, would like to collect in all of them . . . and then start collecting books in hundreds of additional categories, from Allegories to Zoonomia. When it comes to books, I can resist anything but temptation. (Oscar Wilde said that first, but I doubt that he was referring to books.)

As for non-collecting dealers, that other class of the smugly self-possessed: they seem to be a majority. Most whom I know do not collect largely and ostentatiously—although if you press them, some few will admit to having a small, narrowly defined collection of books that are quite different from their specialties as dealers. They tend to be secretive about such matters, because, like all collections, these are nothing less than their minds' mirrors. Therefore, keep away and keep your hands off, for hot breath clouds mirrors and thumb prints smudge them.

And yet, there are a great many dealers, who, while they may not collect now, have gotten where they are (i.e., dealing in old and rare books) through collecting. That is to say, they began as collectors; they collected in innocence, as well as in such areas as fifteenth-century religious tracts, those once-popular yellowbacks sold for railroad travel in nineteenth-century England, first editions of Mark Twain or Petroleum V. Nasby, and eighteenth-century plays. But no matter where they started and what they collected, they eventually became dealers. This is "the natural progression" I referred to earlier. But why should it be natural?

The answer is not difficult. It is natural because when people actively collect a particular author or group of authors or type of book they naturally want to do so intelligently. They want to buy knowledgeably. They want to know things about the area they are collecting in. I refer to such matters as historical data of the period or author(s) in question, along with a broader historical perspective (what is it about Trollope's novels that makes him not only accessible to modern readers, but readable, believable, and useful for our imaginations?), bibliographical facts—including those bibliographical "points" that distinguish one phase of a book's printing history from another—and, of course, the criteria for pricing old and rare books.

Here is where the Devil enters. For if you collect spiritedly, you will work at it. (This work is not really *work*, of course; at least not yet.) You will visit antiquarian bookstores within and without a hundred-mile radius; you will read catalogues issued by dealers in antiquarian books, you will read about your subject, as well as about collecting, generally—sober and informative essays such as this, for example. And as you do these things, a general impression about old and rare books will gradually reveal itself: this can be a very shaggy and wildly uncontrollable market. If you keep your eyes open, you will see prices that appear to fluctuate and vary unpredictably from dealer to dealer.

For example, a book which you have seen advertised in a catalogue for fifty dollars is offered on another dealer's shelf for only ten. Can something be wrong? Well, possibly. You may be faced with what seems to be an opportunity to buy equally valuable copies of the same book for prices that vary five to one. But wait a minute: they may not be copies of the same book at all. They may have the same title, the same binding, the same publication date, the same city named at the bottom of the page . . . and yet be quite different issues or states of the first edition, or even different editions, of the same book. Or perhaps they are indeed the same issue, state, and edition, but (supposing it is a modern book) one is in its original dust jacket, which the other lacks; or perhaps the condition of one is only *good*, whereas the other is *very good*. (These distinctions are meaningful to book people.) Or perhaps one dealer simply judges it to be a more impor-tant title than the other dealer; he or she values it more highly as a literary, historical, artistic, or bibliophilic artifact. There are many factors which could explain honest differences in opinion and the radical disparity in price.

Given all these variables, the first book, advertised in a catalogue, might well be worth the fifty dollars it is priced at, and the second worth only ten. And yet, there could be a genuine bargain here, for booksellers are only human, and they can often be caught dozing when they should be wide awake. They can even be guilty of laziness, premature despair (prolonged bibliographical research can exhaust the most tireless drudge), or casual neglect. The bargain may be the obvious one: both might be worth fifty dollars; or the situation might be reversed, so that the book in the catalogue is overpriced and worth only ten, while the book on the shelf is worth fifty. Then, again, they might both be worth two hundred dollars, or perhaps only four or five. Perhaps just about anything, proving that the concept of worth belongs to that mysterious class of relative abstractions, which also pertains to old paintings, antiques, and—come to think of it— money.[1]

All of these permutations are possible, along with a great many more; and if you are a veteran collector, or if you deal in books, you will have wonderful stories to tell about such matters. I would like to hear them if they are happy stories, featuring your coming upon a first-edition copy of, say, Emerson's *Poems*, published in Boston in 1847, which you bought for a quarter from a surly curmudgeon at a yard sale who didn't even return your greeting when you said hello, and wasn't it a fine day.

That nerdy grumpus deserved to be bilked, and I don't even know him.

❦   Eventually, naturally, as you spend your spare time visiting dealers, studying catalogues, travelling to book fairs, and otherwise pursuing your interests as a collector, you begin to learn that certain books unrelated to your main interest are negotiable. Or perhaps you come across a title you already have in your collection, but that title is radically, breathtakingly, underpriced. Should you pick it up just because it is a good buy?

Here you must move carefully, and very slowly, for this is a dangerous moment. In this context, a good buy can signal a good-by to rational control over one's life. Let us say you purchase this duplicate copy, and take it home and find that it is either in better condition or worse condition than the one you already owned. It makes no difference, for that poorer copy—whichever it might be—is loaded ammunition.

At this juncture, what will a sensible person do? Let's say that you recognize this as a first-edition copy of *Men Without Women*, by Ernest Hemingway (New York, 1927), and you know a dealer who stocks modern first editions. Let's say this is the first issue, and weighs either 15 or 15 ½ ounces (made of heavier paper, therefore heavier than the second issue),

1. And here we all go around acting as if money is a measure instead of a product. Won't we ever learn? Probably not.

and it's better than "good" but not quite "very good" condition. You paid a dollar for it at a flea market, because you saw that it was printed in New York in 1927 and there was no indication of a second printing. You remember that Scribner's later started to encode their first printings with a capital A on the copyright page; but that didn't happen until 1930.

So you made your purchase, got a duplicate copy of *Men Without Women*, and now take it to the dealer. This is theoretically a $400 to $600 book in fine condition, with dust jacket. I say "theoretically," because there has to be a buyer. No doubt there are such buyers; in fact, there are without doubt buyers who would pay $1000 for a spectacularly good copy. But where are they when we need them?

Nevertheless, this is also theoretical—though in another way—for you don't have the dust jacket. So, maybe a plain copy, without dj, is worth $100 to $200; however, yours is not in first-rate condition. All right, $50, then. No, that can't be right, because that would be the dealer's price. The point is—or, to use the familiar, though disgusting, locution—the *bottom line* is, what will the dealer pay you? After all, dealers have overhead costs, stock to replenish, and a profit to make. Besides, as if this weren't enough, the dealer whom you are visiting now happens to have two first-edition copies of *Men Without Women* in stock already, right out there on the shelf in plain sight; one, somewhat worn (though slightly better than yours), is priced at $75 and the other (a tight copy, with bright gold spine label) for $125. Maybe he'd take a hundred for the latter copy; but hold on a minute and get control of yourself: you're selling, not buying.

"I'll give you twenty for it," the dealer says, shooting an index finger at your copy.

"But I thought this was a hundred dollar book!" you cry.

You are then told that, indeed, it may be; but as you can see, there are two unsold copies already in stock—one priced at only $75; so obviously they don't need another copy.

Now you are reduced to a state of ponderous wonderment. And yet, throughout all of this learning process (that's what we call such transactions when they're over), a little voice has been whispering in your head, "But you only paid a dollar for it! Take the twenty and run!"

Nevertheless, you have learned not to listen to this voice with constant attentiveness. This voice can mislead you. As, for example, in the present situation. Because, isn't that a first-edition copy of Hemingway's *Winner Take Nothing* over there on the shelf? No dj, but in very good condition. You open it up and see that it's marked "first edition" in pencil on the front fly leaf, and indeed it does state New York, 1933, at the bottom of the title page, and you turn the title page over and see that, yes, the Scribner A is right in place on the copyright page. Then you turn back and contemplate the front fly leaf, where the dealer's price is clearly marked: $135.

The damnable part of it all is, you don't have a copy of *Winner Take Nothing*. And, of course, you have begun to collect Hemingway, or you wouldn't be here in the first place. In fact, seeing that bright copy makes you realize for perhaps the first time just how much you really do covet Hemingway's first editions. So you stand there and think, while a woman comes in and asks the dealer if there are any Trixie Beldens around, which evokes a commiserative reply that, no, they are out of Trixie Beldens.

So you bite your lip and ponder. You carefully withdraw the copy of *Winner Take Nothing* from the shelf again, and there is that damned A still on the copyright page. "It's a shame it doesn't have a dust jacket," you say in a slow, thoughtful, hesitant voice, just to demonstrate that you know a thing or two, and have high standards.

Finally, you take a deep breath, and the dealer and you get down to some pretty straightforward dealing, so that within another twenty minutes or so, you leave the shop without your copy of *Men Without Women*, but with a first-edition copy of *Winner Take Nothing*, which adds to your Hemingway collection pretty handsomely. After some haggling, the price differential was only $100. You took out your check book and wrote a $100 check, so that, in effect, you got $35 (albeit in trade) for an investment of only $1. You remind yourself that $35 is better than $20, no matter how you look at it.

You feel pretty darned good. You feel good in ways that only another book collector can understand. This is what it's all about, you tell yourself; and you are absolutely right. But then, late that night, when you are lying in bed, with your spouse breathing comfortably and smugly with all the *REM's* anyone could ask for . . . lying there in the darkest part of the night, say at three o'clock—the most difficult hour to be courageous, according to Napoleon—you go over the scene in your head, and suddenly you are aware that the Devil has returned. He has returned to plant the obnoxious weed of a terrible, terrible question in your mind: "What if I'd simply offered a hundred dollars for that book *without any trade?"* If it had been on the shelf for two years, the dealer, being no more than human, might have accepted.

This is of course a question that can never be answered. What if, indeed? But think positively. Wait until morning, then look at your shelf of Hemingway first editions, and see that very good copy (though lacking dust jacket) of *Winner Take Nothing*, and let your mind rest content. Even if the dealer might have accepted an offer of $100 without trade, you're still out only $1.00, and you know you can afford it.

"Yes," a cry resounds deep in your heart, "but that's not the point! I wanted to be shrewd, and now I don't know whether I've been shrewd or not! I may have been *not* shrewd! I may have made a total damned fool of myself!"

Such melodramatics are not often justified, although they are no doubt familiar to most of us. And, as for the scenario just played, let this last consideration bring comfort to you: as you contemplate your first edition of *Winner Take Nothing* on your shelf (containing the first book appearance of "A Clean Well-Lighted Place," don't forget), think of this other fact: that dealer now has three unsold copies of *Men Without Women* , and not a single first edition of *Winner Take Nothing* in stock.

🥝   Think also of something else: you are not alone in the world. I have blundered my way through many such dark and murky transactions as that described above, and so has the dealer who played a major role in our little drama—no matter who he or she is.

I believe that, in the last analysis and far more than we realize, all of us tend to do pretty much what we want to do in life. This is a truth that somehow does not always bring as much comfort as one might think it should. It casts all our failures in a different light, to be sure; but it also changes our successes in slight though inscrutable ways.

Apart from this, however, we do know what a perfect transaction is: it is one in which both parties emerge from the contest with the conviction that each has outdone the other. Or, to put it a little less cynically (and certainly more humanely), both feel they have gotten something of special personal interest and value by trading something less coveted. I would like my partner in trade to be as happy as I am; but of course I want to be happy first, and for what I consider superior reasons.

Already, you will have observed, we have allowed mercantile considerations to sully the purity and ideality of literature. Or of Americana. Or the history of barge travel on the Ohio River, or the history of reports throughout history of objects falling from the sky, or the influence of alcohol consumption upon the settlement of America. Whatever your collecting interest is, it should remain as chaste and inviolate as some mother (any mother will do; think of a sort of miscellaneous mother) in a nineteenth-century melodrama, and should not be troubled by monetary considerations. Especially that sort of monetary consideration that has one eye on making a profit.

At the moment I am speaking of three things: investing in rare books, cant, hypocrisy, gambling, prophecy, pomposity, and silliness. I know that some of you will be ready to point out that there are more than three things in that list. But I don't care: I happen to like the number three, and that's what I'm going to stick with. If you are still troubled, however, you might think of this as *an extra long list* of three things, and be pacified.

There are a lot of people who passionately dislike the idea of investing in rare books. I have found out that many of these people are rich and not very smart. You may be surprised to learn that people can be rich and not very smart, but let me assure you, it is possible. People can be poor and not very smart, too—which is a combination far more often encountered; but then there are many more poor people than there are rich people. To paraphrase Lincoln, God must have loved the poor and not very smart because he made so many of them.

Nevertheless, some rich book collectors who are not in the least slow-witted, but merely selfish, don't want others to think of the investment potential in rare books because they would prefer thinking of such things themselves. They tend to assume a proprietary stance over profits of all sorts, and don't want any meddling from those in the lower socio-economic strata. But deep in their hearts they know that rare books, like just about everything else they can understand, must be paid for; and when the time comes, these same books can be sold; and if there is any justice in the universe, along with a certain amount of taste and shrewdness in their collecting, those books will prove to have appreciated pretty well, if not handsomely, during their years of possession.

Even idealistic scholars sometimes attend to the prices they pay for out-of-print books, and are sometimes aware that occasionally a book they use or need has some status as a rarity. That is to say, it is valuable. It is worth money. It may be worth ten or even a hundred times what this scholar paid for it. I am speaking of monetary gain, and show me the man or woman whose heart will not vibrate to that iron string! A discovery of this sort can indeed, upon occasion, cause a scholar to perk up in ways that do not necessarily relate to the scholarly integrity of his or her chosen subject.

It is a fact that there is still a market for old and rare books in the world, although like everything else under the sun, it is changing. How is it changing? Well, in some areas it has cooled down somewhat—temporarily, I am sure, but measurably. Two obvious reasons for this are the slowing down of inflation (the appreciation in value of rare books is always, to some extent, the obverse of monetary inflation) and the decline in institutional buying, due in part to the recent reign of something called Reagonomics—a neologism that uglifies language and through it part of modern life.

But given the existence of a rare book market (and its poor cousin, the used book market), it is not surprising that many collectors buy with a twofold strategy: directly, to increase their own private collections and, indirectly, to trade duplicate or irrelevant titles with dealers for books in their own collecting areas. Books that are sold rather than traded do not relate to collectors as such; for when this happens, the collector has abandoned his role as collector, and is simply acting as a book scout. There's nothing at all wrong with that, but that's what he or she is, and we might as well call things by their right names, for there is enough confusion in the world already.

Some dealers show signs of being just a little ambivalent about such activities, for—given the generally low liquidity of used books, and even, to a lesser extent, rare books—they would generally prefer cash (a check will do). And yet, most active dealers welcome opportunities to enrich their stock. The single, great, overwhelming problem of antiquarian book dealers is replenishing first-rate stock. Nobody ever has trouble selling good books, but everybody has trouble finding them. These two facts are, of course, related.

But dealers tend to be hospitable for another reason: many, if not most, of them have been on the other side of the counter, as it were, and have spent their apprenticeship collecting and/or scouting. They can well understand, and sometimes even rejoice in, bibliophilic wheeling and dealing. People dropping in with several boxes of books for sale are an important source of supply (especially if they have some understanding of your specialty, and some knowledge of books generally), and should be cherished accordingly. But they can also be the occasion for pleasurable conversation. This is great fun for everybody . . . except for that brief 3 A.M. seizure of anxiety referred to above; but, then, we all suffer such moments, and if you don't wheel and deal in old and rare books, you will find some other cause for anxiety, prodding you awake at 3 A.M., making you knock your head with your knuckles and mutter into your hot damp pillow.

Trading stock is a fascinating and lively enterprise, requiring character, knowledge, bookish instinct, imagination, logic, and passion. And it is naturally accompanied by book talk, which is some of the most interesting talk there is. I can recall weeks, even months, of hours spent with dealers over the years, trading old stories as well as old books. And, while I have gotten many treasures from dealers this way—including my first edition of *Huckleberry Finn*—I have also gotten much that is less tangible. I speak of ideas, gossip, and book lore—rich possessions all.

❧   Of course, there is that ancient housewifely curse pretending to be a question: where are you going to put them? I have often explained and defended my book lust to my wife, relying upon all the arts of persuasion and rationality. She understands, and even participates to some extent, especially on the business side of things. But part of her remains aloof and holds back. I tell her that we live in a world which is not as great or as vast as our imaginations require; I tell her we yearn for absolutes, and should cherish them whenever and wherever found. Then I cite *this* absolute: one cannot possess too many good books.

I believe in that principle, and have often tried to conduct my life according to its dictates and implications. But here we are speaking of an ideal, and as I pointed out earlier, ideals are not meant to be fulfilled; paradoxically, they can tolerate any sort of abuse but fulfillment, for in their fulfillment ideals evaporate.

Had I the means of Sir Thomas Phillipps or Richard Heber, I am convinced that I could prove just as magnificently mad, buying houses, filling them with books, and then buying still more to contain the ever-expanding horde. I would collect everything old and rare, and then spill over into modern first editions. I might not entirely fail in the exercise of taste and character, however; I would draw the line at all post-Civil War textbooks, all book club editions, all modern commercial paperbacks, and maybe all post-1960 documents from the government printing office—although I might have to hedge a bit here and there, for it is conceivable that some paperbacks and government documents might prove very interesting and therefore collectible after all. Not to mention book club editions (BOMC has never clearly articulated their policy in printing stated first editions) and, come to think of it, post-Civil War textbooks—for who wouldn't like to have an 1870 edition of U. S. History published in Idaho or Arizona territory? (So much for character.)

Not having great means, however, I have limited myself to buying a building to house the excess that had begun to interfere with the pleasures of our home. This is not a large building by city, or even small town, standards. It is, in fact, a small building—a single-storey defunct saloon, consisting of approximately 2000 square feet divided unequally into six rooms. It is located in a small economically depressed ex-coal-mining town some thirteen miles away from our home. One factor in our decision to buy it was our estimate of the extreme unlikelihood that books would be stolen in this place; and, while we have suffered some slight vandalism, we have had only one break-in and theft, with only a cheap radio stolen. Conceivably, a few customers have walked out with a book concealed, as they say, on their persons; but I have no proof of this, and am willing to believe that it has not happened.

Vestiges of our building's lively history remain. A large pot-bellied stove was originally the only source of heat, and, given the ten-foot ceilings, there have been winter days when a person could have frozen to death inside almost as easily as outside. (Today it is more efficiently heated.) An old-fashioned, country saloon backbar faces the door some thirty or forty feet away. Upon this backbar, three original beveled mirrors reveal who you are as you approach; and these mirrors are bracketed by oak pillars. The entire backbar is sixteen feet wide and ten feet high. If you stand in a certain spot, you can barely make out the word "Buttermilk" scratched on the surface of the middle mirror. I wondered about this, until I heard that there is a certain stage in the distillation of moonshine whiskey that used to be called buttermilk. If this old backbar could talk, how many stories it could tell . . . stories filled with how much bragging, lying, and just plain down-home ignorance!

When we bought this building, it was in wretched shape, an incipient ruin, so we had it remodelled; and now it has been improved to the extent that it is a serviceable, though stubbornly humble, structure. Soon after shelves were built around the walls, and massive tables that hold eight hundred books each were specially made, the store was surprisingly filled. And this is a state in which it happily remains, even though we have sold many books through the years, and have twice liquidated virtually the entire stock of relatively modern books, selling them to a distant college for their circulation shelves.

At first, we were open to the public every Saturday from May through November, when we could depend on the old stove keeping us alive. My wife would "watch the store," selling books, while I would travel to various household auctions within a fifty- or sixty-mile radius buying more books. Mine was the happier task, for as everyone knows it is much more fun to buy books than sell them. Money is, after all, only money; and people seem to be able to earn it by some pretty disgusting means, which I won't go into at this time.[1]

The store seems to fill by itself. I sometimes wonder if the books don't breed at night, giving birth to baby pamphlets which eventually grow into full bookhood—if not *adult* bookhood—as that term is generally used in

---

1. However, I can't help but point out that there are plenty of books upon all of these subjects, as well as upon the people who collect them.

the seedier downtown sections of big cities. We no longer operate as a store, even on our old leisurely Saturday-only, May-through-November basis—which helps explain the increasing inventory, two virtual liquidations notwithstanding. We often sell to dealers travelling through the area, and have had several special sales for the public as well. We are planning more of these, even though buying is more fun than selling. But I think I just said that.

Our store is not without a colorful history, and some of it may even be true. We are told it has been a barber shop and post office as well as a saloon; and we are also told that at one time there were cockfights and pit bull fights in the basement.[1]

There is a story that one day back in the 1930's a man named Clint Hook was standing in front of the store shooting rats in the creek with his revolver. He was also drunk and feeling mean. Furthermore, Clint Hook was a local cuss, and the sworn enemy (sort of like a sworn deputy, only the other way around) of the town marshall, whose name was Henry Williams. (I know that these names are almost too much; but I can't help it; they're the names given in the story.)

Somebody phoned Henry Williams and told him that Clint Hook was raising hell—shooting rats, breathing hard, making noise, cussing Henry Williams, and being a general all-around sort of nuisance. Henry Williams put on his gun belt, walked to the footbridge that crossed the creek, and stopped when Clint Hook cried out from the other side, "Henry, don't take another step!"

And Henry didn't take another step, at least not right away. What he did was pull his revolver out and shoot Clint Hook dead. Three times, in fact—right in the brisket before his body could hit the dirt. From what they say, you could have laid an octavo, or maybe a quarto, on Clint Hook's chest and covered the spread of those three shots.

This all happened in front of our store, back when it was a saloon or barber shop. Or maybe that was when it was a post office—nobody seems quite sure, and it doesn't make much difference, anyway. Not even to Clint Hook and Henry Williams, who are now just as dead as each other,

---

1. This basement is hardly a basement, but then it certainly isn't an attic; so I don't know what else to call it.

and hardly remembered, except as pale figures in a legendary account of something that happened in front of a building that would some day become a quixotic antiquarian bookstore with the backbar still intact, and the word "buttermilk" still faintly visible, not to mention correctly spelled, if you stand in the right spot and look at it in exactly the right way when it is full daylight.

❦ Since our books are only partially classified, I have been thinking of hanging a sign in our shop, warning the public that they are entering an area of high entropy. It is true that we have half of the shelves on the wall of one room packed exclusively with biography; and we have Americana, westerns, mysteries, and mainstream fiction pretty well clustered in certain other areas of the store. But these are only small, token classifications within a much greater, far more majestic disorder.

Furthermore, even in these little islets of classified books, there is one conventional order lacking, for the books are not arranged alphabetically. And even more distracting than this is the fact that, while there is, for example, a solidly biographical section, not all biographies are in it. And while there is a solid Americana section, much of the Americana is elsewhere. And so it is with westerns and mysteries. Most are lurking in miscellaneous swamps, scattered on other shelves and in other rooms, rubbing shoulders with foreign travel, political histories, trotting horses, and insectivora. It is somewhat as if, in a hardware store, twenty percent of its stock of nuts, bolts, screws, and washers should be selected, then each type (nuts with nuts, and bolts with bolts) put indiscriminately in bins, but without segregating them according to sizes, of either length or diameter—and, most appallingly, leaving that other 80 percent heaped indiscriminately in the remaining bins.

In this way our bookshop is microcosmic, for isn't the world similarly disordered? Don't things fall apart, as Yeats cried out? The center certainly does not hold in our book shop, for it has no center—unless you could think of that large, pot-bellied stove as a center—not an entirely fanciful notion, for our word "focus" derives from the Latin word for "hearth" or "fireplace." But for all the comfort it can bring, a stove cannot be read, much less collected; so I repeat, our store has no center.

It is not even centered in the sense that we specialize in a particular subject or sort of book. While our books are all selected stock (I have bought all with the idea that they are either collectible or otherwise salable), they do not have any particular focus. Or fireplace. Sometimes when I stand in front of the backbar and look at the books surrounding me, I fancy taking a cue from this rich and glorious jumble, and changing the folders in my filing cabinets, labelling all of them "Miscellaneous," and with one bold gesture simplify my files precisely as I complicate my life.

The word "microcosm" itself conveys the idea of order in its last syllable, which is cognate with the word "cosmic," as well as the first syllable in "cosmetologist," or hairdresser. The ancient Greeks thought of the world as an intricately ordered, though very sizable, object. Disorder, which can be defined as "the indefinable," was almost unthinkable to these obsessively rational people; and it was a bold conceit for Anaximander to posit as the fundamental ontological principle, *to apeiron*, which is to say, the "boundless" or indefinable.

It is something of a paradox that our store cannot pretend to be a microcosm of an *orderly* universe; but I believe it does qualify to serve as a model of one of those lesser universes of which that single great one we speak of is, as we hope and used to think, composed. I refer to that universe of old and rare books, and the trade in same. I would argue that an essential part of its fascination lies in its vastness and unpredictability. High entropy? Indeed: but in all of these boundless disorders (I speak of all books, everywhere, in all their confusion) each element, each book, is a tiny cosmos; and many of these are marvels of intricacy, beauty, and power—which is to say, they are *microcosmoi*, or models of order and negentropy. But, macrocosmically, or "mesocosmically," the disorder is grand—so much so that, in spite of my long years of passionate booking, I am still constantly coming upon books I have never seen or heard of before. Or coming upon old and known rarities in extraordinarily unlikely places.

This is of course the great adventure, for adventure and predictability are utterly incompatible. Worse, they are deadly enemies. There can be no adventure without unpredictability. Think of the great age of exploration that began in the fifteenth century; wherever those old sailors ventured, and for whatever reason, they were headed for unpredictability. Furthermore, the printing of books and the age of global exploration began at about the same time; and the two traditions have developed coordinately, one leading eventually to outer space and the other leading to wherever the mind or body can conceive of travelling.

Of course, gold, or the promise of it, enhances exploration. Such titles as Van Allen Bradley's *Gold In Your Attic* and Charles Everitt's *Adventures of a Treasure Hunter* testify to the consensus that not all gold is metallic. In fact, to many of us, it is bibliophilic; and the promise of rare editions combined with the principle of unpredictability provides opportunities for adventure and travel beyond the dreams of unbooked minds.

Lewis Carroll understood this, for think of the world he created for Alice, the Liddell girl he doted upon. The world he made for her was wildly improbable, with logic turned upside down; but the logic was still there, implicit if not manifest. The unpredictability of events in Wonderland was not as great as it might have been, for more often than not, things were simply turned around or pun-pummeled, word-warped, and antic-quaked.

In fine, *Alice in Wonderland* is a book that reminds me of an antiquarian bookstore in which the stock is only partially researched, priced, and classified. And that sort of store is precisely representative of the larger market, where dealer A offers a title for sale that dealer B can buy and sell for a further profit. *No* one knows enough about what is happening. You might as well be Vasco da Gama or Lewis and Clark, for all your past experience can help.

And, given these facts, is it any wonder that we blunder so delightedly and with such panache? Who knows where what will appear? Who even knows what what is? All that we can be sure of is, what we eventually find will be worth finding and it will be in print. And whoever cannot understand the adventure of all this simply doesn't know what's what.

❦ *In Search of*
Unreadable Books

Though my title may not be entirely disingenuous, I assure you that I am not playing a game at the first level. That is to say, my subject is not that class of books which are intended to be viewed rather than read. Of course, pictorial books are a worthy subject, for many are superb productions, therefore obviously collectible. Examples that immediately come to mind are John Trusler's two-volume edition of *The Works of William Hogarth* (London, 1833) or F.T. Miller's 10 volume *Photographic History of the Civil War* .

The central attraction of such books is explicitly, unmistakably, visual; one possesses them because of their plates, not their prose style, much less anything like character development or intricacy of plot. Plates cannot provide anything like a true intricacy of plot, not even in Hogarth's most famous production, "The Rake's Progress," showing, if not telling, the stages in the eighteenth century's version of a descent into decadence.

Nevertheless, while such books as these may be said to exist primarily for their plates, their texts—though subordinate—are not necessarily unreadable. And often much of the interest to be found in books of plates lies in the text itself, which can convey so much beyond the scope of pictures: time, situation, intent, and biographical and historical information concerning both subjects and artist or photographer. Truly, a few well-chosen words can be worth 10,000 pictures.

Actually, they can be worth infinitely more, as, in some such notation from another context: "When this photograph (his most famous) was taken, Poe had just emerged from the hospital, where he had been given large doses of laudanum." An entire library of pictures could not convey even 1/24th of the information in this sentence of twenty-four words, except indirectly (as in rebus writing), which is to say, by means of language equivalence, in the manner of translating verbal meanings into some far less precise form of crude pictorial representation. But of course, even this would prove a sad translation, woefully inadequate to the text.

But my subject does not have to do with "picture books"; it has to do with books that are unreadable not because they are not primarily *meant* to be read, but because the books are simply bad. The text itself is bad. The writing is ineffectual, muddle-headed, trivial, insubstantial, dull, under-invented . . . *awful.* I am speaking of virtually worthless books, as judged by almost any conceivable literary, scientific, or scholarly standard.

One would think that examples are plentiful, and of course this must be true; however, such examples are not as accessible for reference as one might think, because the books we are speaking of are almost by definition easily forgotten. Think of the challenge in being asked the title of the most forgettable book you have ever read.

But in this region of chaos and old night, there are books that are characterized by more than mediocrity or uselessness. Some books are so godawful bad, they achieve a sort of excellence in godawfulness, which has to be a measure of something, even if it extends in the wrong direction. "Superlatively, incomparably awful." Here is a label that one might almost take pride in. It certainly possesses the virtue of extremity, and we are inclined to honor extremes of almost any sort in this simple-minded, thrill-oriented era of "the bottom line," *The Guinness Book of Records*, and Trivial Pursuit.

Julia Moore, "The Sweet Singer of Michigan," was an ostentatiously awful writer, and upon those few occasions when she is remembered or quoted, she is quoted in a spirit of contumelious merriment. Her *The Sentimental Songbook* (Grand Rapids, 1876) is judged to be a $100 book by Van Allen Bradley in the 3rd edition of his *Handbook of Values* . (If you cannot gain a literary reputation one way, do it in the opposite; a century from now, it may be hard to tell the difference.) And I have written elsewhere[1] about "Count Coffinberry," the Ohio lawyer, whose utter, uncompromising ineptitude as a poet has seldom, perhaps never, been surpassed. Not even by the Sweet Singer herself.

I have come upon another volume of verse that falls in this class, although it does not sink quite so deep, and my discovery of it was rather

1. In "Books and Learning on the Old Frontier, God Help Us," published in *Booking in the Heartland* (Johns Hopkins, 1986).

curious. In fact, I sought out this book with considerable effort, after reading a passage in one of William Butler Yeats' autobiographical works, *The Trembling of the Veil* (monumentally *not* an unreadable book, for in my judgment Yeats' gift for prose is nearly condign with his gift for poetry). Yeats is speaking of Edwin Ellis, a friend of his early youth, who was both painter and poet:

> He was . . . sometimes moving as a poet and still more often an astonishment. I have known him cast something just said into a dozen lines of musical verse, without apparently ceasing to talk; but the work once done, he could not or would not amend it, and my father thought he lacked all ambition. Yet he had at times nobility of rhythm—an instinct for grandeur, and after thirty years I still repeat to myself his address to Mother Earth—
>
> > O mother of the hills, forgive our towers,
> > O mother of the clouds, forgive our dreams.
>
> And there are certain whole poems that I read from time to time or try to make others read. There is that poem where the manner is unworthy of the matter, being loose and facile, describing Adam and Eve fleeing from Paradise. Adam asks Eve what she carries so carefully, and Eve replies that it is a little of the apple core kept for their children.[1]

When I first read this passage, it blazed on the page, and thereafter I couldn't put it from my mind. The preceding couplet is good enough, true; but the conception that Yeats paraphrases at the end of the quoted section seems wonderful to me, and in spite of Yeats' implicit warning, I couldn't believe that this sample might inhabit a poor poem.

I looked for Ellis' work in our university library, where it was not to be had, so I then tapped out a message on OCLC (our computerized inter-library listing), and found that there was, indeed, a copy of *Fate in Arcadia and Other Poems* , London, 1892, that could be procured by inter-library loan. I filled out the proper request, waited the two weeks for the book's arrival, and then when it arrived, eagerly pitched myself into one of the

1. *The Autobiography of William Butler Yeats*, NY (1965), pp. 107-8.

great miseries of English poesy. I couldn't even find that episode that Yeats refers to; but perhaps, having read what seemed to be the first four or five thousand pages, I was so stultified I wasn't able to recognize it, if it was, in fact, there. It is possible, also, that I'd even gotten the wrong book, although I couldn't find a likely alternative . . . and even if I could, after that brief exposure to Ellis' verse, I would not look for it.

Although we have Yeats' word that the conception was Ellis', its full poetic force was not realized until Yeats saw it, plucked it from the grime, and gave it casual allusive paraphrase and distillation, knowing a good poetic idea when he saw one, and also knowing when "the manner was unworthy of the matter." It was Yeats' great gift as a poet that took him to this anecdote, his mind a dousing rod that made his head nod yes at that instant, when all around there seemed to be nothing but arid desert, the parched soil filled with cockles and burrs and the weeds of mediocrity.

❦   While I did not stay with *Fate in Arcadia* long enough to savor it in all its wretchedness, there are books that I have read in their entirety, and with something like self-satisfaction, if not pride. Sometimes, as in laboratory experiments, negative results are as welcome as positive. There are occasions when we simply need information, and if we feel strongly about it, we will read a great deal to get it.

I know of no more inspiring example of the dogged pursuit for a clue than that provided by John Livingston Lowes in his triumphant work of scholarship, *The Road to Xanadu: A Study in the Ways of the Imagination*, Boston, 1927. While in college, I read this book with what must have been something like the wild surmise that Keats felt upon reading Chapman's translation of Homer. It is a great and powerful scholarly accomplishment, and so fascinating from beginning to end that I can still feel its potency, forty years after having read it.

Lowes' purpose was to trace all of Coleridge's reading in search of images and ideas that were to appear—either transformed or whole—in Coleridge's two most famous poems. "I propose," he wrote, "to tell the story, so far as I have charted its course, of the genesis of two of the most remarkable poems in English, 'The Rime of the Ancient Mariner' and 'Kubla Khan.' " The words that will interest us in this context are "so far as I have charted its course"—for that course was great and not easily charted. Coleridge was not only what is called "an omnivorous reader," he was remarkably careless and impetuous in his personal habits (those who loaned books to him regretted it) as well as in his manner of reading.

But Lowes was worthy of his subject. Somewhere out of his own breadth of knowledge, he connected certain images of luminescence in "The Ancient Mariner" with what he knew of Joseph Priestley's treatise on *Opticks*, published in 1772. Coleridge knew and admired Priestley's work, so the likelihood was great; but responsible, old-fashioned scholars cannot rest content with mere likelihood, no matter how likely. Therefore, Lowes set about to see if he could find evidence that Coleridge had read this "ponderous quarto of eight hundred and twelve pages."

From here on, it is best to let Lowes tell the story in his own words:

> With the Note Book [Coleridge's] pretty definitely in my head, I began on the *Opticks*, and plodded doggedly through eight hundred and six obsolete pages of the heroic dimensions of those unhurried days, still nursing the unconquerable hope that a jewel might at any moment turn up in the dustheap. But the eight hundred and six pages were as bare of a clue as the palm of my hand. The eight hundred and seventh completed the text. I turned the page before it with a sigh of relief; that job, at least, was done! And there, on the very last page of the text, before my weary but not yet quite disillusioned eyes, stood this:
>
>> Dr. Franklin shewed me that the flames of two candles joined give a much stronger light than both of them separate; as is made very evident by a person holding the two candles near his face, first separate, and then joined in one.
>
> I was not at all sure that the statement was correct. I do not know now, for I have never put it to the test. But what I did know was this—that on the very first page of [Coleridge's] Note Book were rather illegibly scribbled these words:
>
>> The flames of two Candles joined give a much stronger light than both of them separate—evid. by a person holding the two Candles near his Face, first separate, and then joined in one.[1]

1. pp. 38, 39. (Five pages comprise a list of technical terms.)

I do not mean to imply that Priestley's book is in any important way "unreadable"; Priestley's is one of the great names in physical science. . . ; which does not in itself mean that everything he wrote is readable, but it certainly does not suggest that one of his titles might not be. However, within the scope of Lowes' purpose, much of *Opticks* must have proved uninteresting; and I would like to think that he did some judicious scanning, here and there, even though the issue can no longer be considered a very urgent one—the world being what it is, and Lowes being long dead, and his travail with Priestley past.

The labels "readable" and "unreadable" do not, of course, refer to facts, but to judgments. And judgments are always functions of the opinions, principles, needs, moods, and quirks of individual readers at particular times. What is unreadable today, may prove wonderfully interesting tomorrow. Or *vice versa*. Years ago, a friend of mine, who had read W. Somerset Maugham's *Of Human Bondage* with such admiration when he was eighteen years old that exactly twenty years later—with a sort of ritualistic piety—he decided to reread the book, only to find it sadly disappointing. Had he aggrandized it so much in his memory that no book could have proved worthy? Perhaps. Or had he somehow "outgrown" the book? Maybe. Whatever the truth of the matter, we have here an example of a book that would seem to have been proved both readable and unreadable by the same reader; except for the fact that it wasn't the same reader at all, the two of him being separated by twenty years.

❦   Books do not have to be "bad" to be unreadable. If you are spending an afternoon on the beach, in the mood for a good detective story, *The Spoils of Poynton* or *The Magic Mountain* might well prove unreadable. Like all judgments, this is situational and intricate in its factors, and it is only at the most splendid extreme that books seem to be categorically unreadable. Even Julia Moore is readable today, although the reasons for this are hardly of the sort that could have given comfort, much less pride, to "The Sweet Singer of Michigan."

What motivates us to throw our time away upon hopeless books? There are different motives: some people finish a book they have begun as a matter of honor—my wife is one of these. I sympathize, in a way, and always feel a little diminished when I toss a book aside, having read ten or twenty pages, then giving up in despair. Like all readers, I passionately *want* books to be good; I want to be entertained, informed, edified, entranced. I want to learn something from each, even if the author's purpose in writing it is avowedly undidactic.

But sometimes we go to a book without expecting amusement or edification in the larger sense; we go to it for information. People don't read books on changes in tax laws or on real estate investment (or *think* they don't) for the style, but to be informed. And plain information is possessed of its own dignity and interest. Aristotle claimed that human beings "by nature" desired to know; and we keep hoping he is right.

Several years ago I undertook to seek out the truth about Grosset and Dunlap. Book collectors and dealers will know what I am talking about. The great question is: in spite of Grosset and Dunlap's ostensibly explicit commitment to reprinting titles first brought out by other publishers, isn't it possible that they actually, upon occasion, published real first editions? I have discussed this with many book people, and the majority seem to suspect that some G&D titles might be true first editions. Some even claim it for a fact.

So I decided to read George T. Dunlap's autobiography, *The Fleeting Years*, which was published in 1937. I read every page, alert for the slightest clue that now and then Grosset and Dunlap had sneaked a first printing into their line . . . and if I had gotten this information, I would have had an opportunity to be shrewd when others were not. (Book collectors and dealers will have difficulty understanding this attitude, but I state it in the interest of truth.)

Not only did I read the entire book, but I read it with the vague memory not only of those who suspected what I suspected (*surely*, in all that mountain of books published by G & D there would be at least *one* first edition slipped in!), but also of having once, years ago, seen a copy of *Lady Chatterly's Lover*, published by Grosset and Dunlap and clearly stating "First American Edition" on the copyright page. (Since then, I have consulted bibliographies without finding any reference to this fact, although the bibliographical features of Lawrence's most shocking book are a stew of information.)

The ghosts of vague memories did not help, however. George T. Dunlap did not once refer to printing a first edition of anything. He made generous reference to many of the reprints undertaken by his company since its formation in 1897, but that was all. On the other hand, his statements did not amount to anything like an explicit affirmation that G & D had *never* brought out a first; he simply, consistently, implied that they had not . . . and yet, the language in such areas turned a little soft, I thought, so that my suspicions are still not completely laid to rest.

Thus I emerged from the book as ignorant as I had entered it. And, yes, Dunlap's autobiography is pretty much in the unreadable class. I do not recommend it for amusement or edification either one. Perhaps for a demonstration of one's sturdiness of character in undertaking it, but that is all.

🦇   This brings us, by mysterious paths, to Calvin Coolidge. America's most taciturn president has become a figure of fun, and we need all the fun we can get—especially when the object of our ridicule is long dead. What harm is there in it? Hardly any at all, beyond the perpetuation of a certain natural human viciousness.

Coolidge has entered our folklore secretly, after dark, by the back gate, so that he looms upon some fringe in the past like a minor comic political figure and a pretty nothing sort of president. Probably he is best known for two things: his general reputation for silence (or when things got too hot, an occasional laconic utterance) and the remark that Dorothy Parker was supposed to have made in 1933, when she was seated with that famous group of *littérateurs* at the Algonquin Club, and it was announced that ex-President Coolidge had died. "How can they tell?" she asked.

But somewhere I came across another story, one in which he has a more specific presence. The scene for this story is a formal banquet, where, when all in the party had taken their places at the table, the woman seated beside Coolidge said, "Oh, Mr. President, everybody bet me that I wouldn't get three words out of you this evening!" To which, Coolidge answered, "You lose."

Not bad at all, but not the sort of thing to send someone in search of

Coolidge's *obiter dicta* . . . not in the same league as poor maternal loving Eve with her bit of the apple saved for the children. But then, somewhat later (where, I have no idea), I read that once when he was asked about his taciturnity, Coolidge said, "If you don't say something, you won't be asked to repeat it."

Now this is something. It is a joke that engages ontological as well as epistemological matters. What, in short, is the antecedent of "it"? Yes, these are deep matters, and that is a wonderfully witty reply. It stuck with me; I thought about it. Thinking about it made me realize how important the antecedents of pronouns are. If someone says, "It is getting cold out" or "It's past ten o'clock," what exactly does the pronoun *it* refer to? (Note: if you answer "air" to number one, and "time" to number two, you're only partly right, and it's the other part that bothers me.)

Such deep thoughts got me to reciting an old conundrum (source also unknown, like so much in my life):

> For he thought it was she,
> And she thought it was he;
> But when they got closer to each other,
> They realized it was neither one of them.

Still, I like Coolidge's better. It's drier, shrewder, and less fancy. What was this fellow like? I was curious about a man who could say such a thing and yet be so mocked by fast-talking mediacrats—whenever they mentioned him at all, that is. I have often seen Coolidge's book, *Have Faith in Massachusetts*—which is an intriguing title, especially in view of the fact that Coolidge was from Vermont—but I have not read it beyond its title.

"If you don't say something, you won't be asked to repeat it." That utterance kept repeating itself in my head until finally I gave up and sought out Coolidge's Autobiography, published in 1929, while he was still alive. Somewhere in those pages, I reasoned, a cool and wry intelligence would become manifest. It was almost a certainty, because I was looking for it; and if you look for something, your chances of finding it are greatly increased. I began reading it with something of the wary alertness of one who is intent upon cracking a code, for I knew that whatever humor might exist, would exist beneath some superficial solemnity that would look and sound presidential. I knew how unlikely it would be to expect gags, puns, and some stylistic equivalent of whoopie cushions, supposing there is one.

In this, I was correct. There were indeed no gags, no puns, no whoopie cushions. In fact, there was no humor at all. It was the sort of book Dorothy Parker would have expected Coolidge to write, and it was so utterly in character with his public image, that I suspect it was ghost written. It was stern, prudent, pious, restrictive, and dull. Here was a book that should be prominent in anyone's list of unreadable books. "But what did you expect?" most people would ask. Yes, but those are not the people who are familiar with that noble sentence: "If you don't say something, you won't be asked to repeat it."

This sentence is good enough to have been written by Ulysses S. Grant, who, in his *Memoirs*, states that when he was a boy he'd heard so often that a noun was the name of a thing, he eventually believed it. James Norman Schmidt—a writer, colleague at Ohio University, and cherished friend—years ago told me he suspected that Twain himself had taken a part in the writing of Grant's great two-volume work. Although this is an attractive idea, I have never seen any evidence to support it. But whatever the truth of that, we must not stray farther; and, anyway, I am utterly certain that Twain had nothing to do with Coolidge's autobiography.

What *about* Calvin Coolidge? Did he suffer only two seizures of mirth during a lifetime of spartan public service? Or did he live a secret life, as we all do, content to be thought an earnest mediocrity, a thrifty dullard, and a colorless killjoy . . . while somewhere deep inside, beyond the purview of publicity, a shrewd, honest, truth-bitten Yankee farmer lived a life of wry perspicacity?

The question seems trivial, but I insist that it is not. It raises a question of character, and is therefore not nearly as silly as most of what passes for politics. It is as important, in its way, as the problem of the antecedence of the pronoun "it"; and I do not propose to let it drop. So what if Coolidge's death was the occasion for a brief yack at the Algonquin? So what if Theodore Roosevelt's daughter, Alice Longworth, said that Coolidge looked like a man who'd been weaned on a pickle?

What would the press of today have done with someone like Calvin Coolidge? They would have missed seeing him altogether, and I suspect that their grandfathers in journalism managed it almost as well as they would have done. Journalists are limited by what Thorstein Veblen called "trained incapacity"—just as we all are, indeed; but there has to be a watchdog for the press, so that what is reflected from its presumptions and obsessions (e.g., the selection of news by its thrill-factor and then packaging it in daily amounts for public consumption) does not pass unchallenged for truth.

Coolidge may have understood this; then again, he may have not. It is a truth that may have become evident after his time; but aside from that, it is difficult to assess how much he really did understand. He was the most inscrutable of public figures, and it is no wonder he is forgotten and despised, for what the media can't pry open is generally assumed not to exist at all. His attitude toward journalists was not, as they say today, "confrontational"—at times he had something of the severe avuncular affection of a crusty old schoolmaster. The entire press conference entry for Nov. 13, 1923, quotes him as saying: "The class doesn't seem to be so inquisitive this morning as it sometimes is. There isn't a very large crop of questions."

But elsewhere, he appears to agree with his one-time friend, Will Rogers, who is said to have said, "All I know is what I read in the newspapers." Coolidge's comments often sound a bit distant and wistful, as if he's half afraid his subscription is about to run out. He was aware of the power of the press—although hardly as obsequious as politicians today—so that he could twit them when he was so inclined. Discussing plans at a press conference for giving a Memorial Day address at Gettysburg, Coolidge asked about the best way to get there. Should he go by train or car? The train was suggested, and of course the gentlemen of the press would accompany him. To which suggestion Coolidge replied sardonically: "With the press aboard, I take it that the railroad would be solicitous in getting us there."

Generally, however, his relationship with the press was one of mutual benefit. The journalistic values of today are such that his image would probably not even be visible—that is to say, not an image at all; and it is to some extent through those values that all of us have to try to see him—which makes him such a pale and harmless-seeming ghost hovering somewhere at the edge of our political history. Of course, the press of his day should have been somewhat better able to cope with him, and possibly even appreciate him, than today's would have been, for they all shared the same time, the same culture, the same *Weltanschauung*—to use a strikingly unCoolidgean word.

It was Herbert Hoover who established the office of press secretary. Before him, Coolidge gave press conferences, of course, but he spoke for himself, and answered only questions that had been put in writing. His answers were often not answers at all, but sly evasions or forthright confessions of ignorance, depending upon your point of view. Still, in addition to this, they were sometimes salted with a wit so dry that it might have been inaudible under the sound of scribbling pencils.

❧   Much of what I have just written serves as evidence that I did not give up on Calvin Coolidge. His entire autobiography is hardly as revealing as the preceding two paragraphs, although it is considerably more inspirational, in a general way, and more earnestly promotive of industry, honesty, and thrift. The autobiography, in short, was not enough; that single utterance would not leave me alone. Like John Livingston Lowes, I was infatuated by a notion, a hunch—his having to do with Coleridge, mine with Coolidge. Even the names are much alike.

The next step in my quest took me to a book titled, *The Talkative President: the Off-The-Record Press Conferences of Calvin Coolidge* , edited by Howard H. Quint and Robert H. Ferrell, published by the University of Massachusetts Press, Amherst (1964). My battle cry was "Have Faith in Massachusetts!" (or at least their university press) and I am prepared to believe what this book reports. The Foreword was written by Lyle C. Wilson, and it begins: "Calvin Coolidge was the contriver of the most persistent and transparent political hoax of twentieth-century America. He effected it by speaking to the American people twice weekly from his White House press conference forum through the medium of 'the White House Spokesman.' I was a party to the hoax. So were a dozen or more of my news colleagues."

Now this was more like it! Here was a man, I thought, who'd seen through the pale actuary of morals (that photo of Coolidge wearing an Indian headdress wouldn't fool a child today—not when we have so much verisimilitude built into our plastic toys. Here was a man who'd *caught on.*

Well, I thought that way for several paragraphs, but when I'd finished the Foreword, I wasn't quite clear about what that "most persistent and transparent political hoax" *was*. Did it have to do with Wilson's statement that Coolidge's remarks were jotted down and then reported as having been uttered—not by the President, himself—but "a White House Spokesman"? There's hardly enough hoax in that to turn a page. Furthermore, it's unthinkable that Coolidge was the first president whose words were filtered through a bureaucratic hedge. And beyond that, Coolidge didn't *say* all that much, so where's the problem?

Wilson does mention that Coolidge's "press conferences were a forum for sly, wry humor, as the selections in Chapter I indicate." This is welcome news, but it has no stated counterpoise necessary for it to stand as a "hoax." It is embarrassing to miss a promised reference to the "most persistent and transparent political hoax of the twentieth century"; and I am ashamed of myself, along with being inclined to believe one of three things: 1) the hoax was not Coolidge's at all, but Mr. Wilson's on us; 2) Mr. Wilson was distracted somewhere in the writing of his Foreword and forgot what he'd promised at the beginning; 3) the Foreword was written by Calvin Coolidge (there are touches of his style in it), given to Mr. Wilson with the solemn charge that he never make it public unless some such book as this were written long after his death.

Of the three, I like the last best; but of course I have nothing whatsoever to substantiate the charge, and hereby withdraw it. The Foreword is not of the "unreadable" variety, however; and it does not give evidence that the book to follow will prove unreadable. The Foreword is not unreadable or dull, it is merely perplexing. Nevertheless, it says interesting things about Coolidge's press conferences. In addition to that, it introduces Coolidge's secretary (not "press secretary"), who was a man with the wonderful name of C. Bascom Slemp. Of him, Mr. Wilson says, "Slemp was a Virginia politician whose funereal appearance and melancholy air may have come of his lifelong effort to proselyte his native state, Virginia, for the Republican Party."

Well, any text that generates questions is worthy, in its way, and the sample given above should be sufficient to demonstrate that this is a not unworthy book upon whose brink we are poised . . . which is certainly as much as you can expect from a Foreword that is only slightly more than two pages in length. Therefore, it is time that we get to the main feast, which is Silent Cal, The Talkative President himself, and what he is said to have said.

❦   While people are always complaining of being "quoted out of context," the fact is that the dignity of language is such that it is often the case that utterances out of context are more eloquent than many fully equipped with context.

In the *present* context, we are presented with paragraphs and sentences that all seem to have been plucked from something larger. Indeed, I would argue that texts that we judge to have literary merit are identifiable precisely by this measure—that they convey a sense of a much richer reality than is denoted . . . which is to say, they *always* give an impression of being somewhat out of context. The ratio of implied, or sensed, meaning to the explicit is an index to a work's fullness, its richness, its literary worth. I believe that this is a factor in our understanding of the genius implicit in the plain style, in contrast to the gorgeous, baroque stylistic display of, say, William Faulkner or Sir Thomas Browne. They, too, will convey far more than their minimal significations; but the richness of their surface texture is such that the disparity between it and implicit meaning is not so radical that we are aware of it.

Thus it is that *The Talkative President* (gamey title, there) reads somewhat like a chrestomathy or commonplace book. But there is an important difference, for honesty insists that I tell you that much of what is quoted is "unextractable," in the sense that it will not amuse, titilate, or beguile a totally uninterested, or even disinterested, reader.

Largely, this has to do with the matters addressed. No matter how sly and whimsical Coolidge was, or might have been, he could not fail to address dull topics with appropriate answers. Who wants gags from a president when the ship of state is sinking? Or *seems* to be sinking? Wit is all right in its place, but it can lead an earnest politician astray, as Adlai Stevenson discovered. And when Coolidge is not being witty in his answers, he is the featureless figure of almost forgotten memory: cautious, fair-minded, cautious, prudent, cautious, thorough, and cautious.

But this is not what we are in search of—like John Livingston Lowes, we are reading selectively, tendentiously. We are looking for something special—not slimy images or those relating to the synergism of candle flames—but instances of wit. And, unlike his autobiography (written by a ghost writer only slightly more vital than Bartleby, the Scrivener, I suspect), there are many instances in this book; and I am happy to report that they reveal the man who once said that which does not need saying again, since I have repeated it two or three times already, and while repetition may be the Mother of Learning (as the old Schoolmen repeated so often: *Repetitio est Mater Studiorum*), I have learned that it can be done too often.

The most singular characteristic of Calvin Coolidge's remarks to the press are his insistence upon how little he knows. (One can only wish that contemporary politicians were so Socratically wise.) Take, for example, pages 142 and 143, facing each other, as is only proper. Six out of his seven reports convey something in the way of helpless ignorance. They begin with the following sentences: 1) "No information has come to me concerning the increase in rediscount rates, except that which I have seen from the press." 2) "I have no information relative to proposed legislation about loans on securities." 3) "I have very little information about the investigation going on before the Federal Trade Commission relative to the electric power companies." 4) "I haven't seen the Muscle Shoals bill and know but very little about it." 5) "I haven't a great amount of information concerning the business situation, but I was advised this morning by the Department of Commerce that the last six months, according to their reports, was better than the first six months of the year 1928 and was up to the standard of 1927." 6) "So far as I know it is a very good idea of the Interstate Commerce Commission to direct Commissioner [Claude R.] Porter to prepare a plan for the unification of the railroads."

The last is the most informed of the six quoted, but it shows judicious hedging; and of course I haven't quoted the seventh comment because in it Coolidge quite uncharacteristically gives a straight, informed, no-nonsense answer relating to a veto message he had delivered. I should state that these facing pages were not selected out of a process of careful screening—they are representative, although perhaps a little less communicative than the average. I should also point out that they were delivered in late 1928 and in January, 1929—shortly before Hoover became president and within a year of the great Stock Market crash of 1929.

Ignorance can have its charms, else who amongst us could be happy? And yet, ignorance so relentlessly admitted can be disturbing, especially when it comes in messages from the President of the United States. But of course, one has to understand the game of politics, much in the same way one learns to play those other games, including that of life itself.

Nevertheless, one also has to be impressed by the testimony given in this book. Coolidge didn't simply admit to not knowing something, he appeared to enjoy it. Few people seem to have gotten so much pleasure out of confessing ignorance; and this fact alone sets him apart. Was he some sort of political atavism, a 1920's version of a Know Nothing? Or was he a Vermont Socrates, stuck in Washington by an ironic fate, unaware of how one could buy a bus ticket back to Vermont? Whatever the answer, one thing is evident: this is a man who deserves closer scrutiny. How much there was he didn't say!

🐝 Very early in the text of *The Talkative President*—on page 2, in fact—we are told about this—how much Coolidge did not tell, how many important issues there were that he simply did not officially acknowledge and may have known little, or cared little, about. "In some instances one seeks almost in vain, and in others totally so, for presidential pronouncements on such matters as the Harding scandals, prohibition, the Sacco-Vanzetti case, the Ku Klux Klan, labor unions, the movies, radio, welfare capitalism [*sic*], the Scopes Trial, bank failures, the Florida real estate boom, and last, but not least, the New York Stock Exchange's rampaging bull market."

Well, what *was* Coolidge thinking about? Did he think at all? Of course he did, but evidently he didn't think about things, even "critical things," the way politicians and the rest of us are supposed to think. The list of issues he appeared to ignore is impressive, and strengthens the similarities one inevitably finds between Coolidge and Eisenhower, and even to a somewhat lesser extent—Ronald Reagan.

In some ways, Coolidge seemed to have had the soul of an actuary . . . albeit one with both a wit and a conscience. Not only did he say that the business of America was business (tuning a fine equivocation into that innocent utterance), but he said that "Economy is idealism in its most practical form." (Our editors label that as "banal," but I think it just misses . . . depending, of course, upon exactly how it is meant; I find something a bit inscrutable in it, but then I'm the one who couldn't even figure out what the hoax mentioned in the Foreword was.)

Whatever the state of his conscience, it seems clear how he liked to spend his time. "Coolidge balanced the budget and obtained a surplus. As day after day the President sat in his White House office, feet on the desk and cigar in mouth, looking over piles of reports, he read fiscal papers with an especially sharp eye. He considered government economy in terms of personal economy—a government debt was analogous to a private debt."

These are interesting matters, but I have to keep reminding myself that my subject is not Coolidge's effectiveness as a government servant, much less his place in history. I am in search of the man who said you know what. So let us return to this, our proper concern, and contemplate the following exchange:

PRESS: Was there a Cabinet meeting today?
PRESIDENT: Yes, but there was practically no business transacted at
   the Cabinet meeting. It only lasted about 15 minutes, after which
   the world will soon know that we had our picture taken.

This was on Sept. 11, 1923. On Sept. 26 of the next year, the same question was asked, and the Press was informed that a case of hoof and mouth disease had been discovered in Texas. "As soon as it was established," Coolidge said, "it was taken care of."

His wit is certainly not ostentatious, as these examples show; but there is an undercurrent of whimsy that is far subtler and more resonant intellectually than the celebrated quips of John F. Kennedy, most of which can be seen as humorous only through a willing suspension of disbelief or a mental reminder that this is the President of the United States talking and thinking he's really being funny.

When in Superior, Wisconsin, on Aug. 7, 1928, Coolidge was asked about his immediate plans, and answered as follows:

> I am expecting to go over to Duluth some day. I think they are planning a sort of drive for me around there. I don't know just when I shall go. I have been so busy out at the Lodge catching fish—there are 45,000 out there—I haven't caught them all yet, but I have them all pretty well intimidated. They have had to restock one lake.

Then, still in Superior almost a month later, the following exchange took place (the President talking):

> I think the press already knows that I am expecting to attend the Fair—tomorrow, isn't it, Mr. Sanders?
>
> MR. SANDERS: Yes, tomorrow afternoon about 2:00 o'clock.
> MR. YOUNG: It isn't likely you will say anything tomorrow at the Fair?
> PRESIDENT: No. I am just going as an exhibit.

Ten days after this, still in Superior (he was good in Wisconsin and evidently had faith in it), he sustains this particular sort of whimsy, as follows:

> I think the idea that I might go hunting in Kentucky arose from the fact that the bird dog that was given me in Superior I had Colonel Starling send down to a friend of his in Kentucky, who is a very fine trainer of dogs. I presume that all the hunting I will do in Kentucky will be done by proxy through this dog.

These are only some of the good things I find in this book, but they do not quite live up to the promise implicit in that first prompting. But then, hope usually outdistances fulfillment, as we all learn in one way or other. And yet, hope is always to some extent present, which is in itself the occasion for hope.

Through all of this, my sense of Calvin Coolidge has been enriched. (It is something to be able to say that you have read his Autobiography; try it in polite company some time.) Nevertheless, I am not sure that I understand a great deal more about him than I did before. I simply have more information to confuse myself with. But . . . no, that is too easy and pessimistic. I can understand things about him that I did not understand before; and one of the greatest of these is the realization that—Dorothy Parker notwithstanding—there was probably a very complex man who became president of this country, even though he was also a rather simple ex-country boy from Vermont. Two complexities together—like two candle flames merged—are impressive; but when you have complexity joined to simplicity, then you *really* have something that's complicated!

Simplicity and complexity are transactionals, so it is hardly astonishing to have one insist that both of these things are possible, packed together in one rather colorless human package. It is easy to understand that he was never adequately represented by what he said or did . . . not even representable by some theoretically sum total of all these things. Which is to say, Coolidge might have been a little bit like you and me.

In view of this fact, and in view of the principle that it is always good to end with an opening, I can't think of a better way to end my essay than by quoting one of his characteristic opening statements—this one part of his answer to a question put by the press. By now, the words should be familiar to you; and they are, as you will see, utterly appropriate, as follows: "I don't know of anything I can say more about the return of alien property than what I said the other day."

You may have been a little surprised by that "alien property" business, but the rest should be clear. "I don't know of anything I can say more." There is an old-timey kind of music in those words, and we should listen to them carefully. The world would be better off if more of us understood their fundamental though mysterious dignity. Of course, I don't really, entirely *believe* those words for a minute; but then you have to stop somewhere. And I propose to do so right now, at this instant, because if I say anything else, I might be asked to repeat it.

🍎 Hodgson's Island

"Authors of the eighteenth century delighted in copious subtitles. These had one signal merit; they saved the reader further trouble." So begins Walter de la Mare's, *Desert Islands and Robinson Crusoe* (London, 1930; No. 7 of The Rose and Crown Library), which is itself a volume that has no subtitle at all.

Playfully, however, immediately following the two sentences quoted above, the author provides that which *might* have been a subtitle, which reads as follows: *"DESERT ISLANDS:* being the *VOYAGE* of a *HULK,* called by courtesy a *Lecture,* that was launched under the Auspices of *The Royal Society of Literature* of *London* many years ago, namely, in 1920, was afterwards frequently in Dock again for Repair and then refitted for FARTHER ADVENTURINGS, and so at length became laden with an unconscionable Cargo of Odds and Ends and Flotsam and Jetsam, much of it borrow'd from other Vessels infinitely more Seaworthy than itself, and the most of that concern'd with what are known as ISLANDS, some of them Real, some of them Allegorical, and the rest purely Fabulous. . . ."

Well, you get the idea. This hypothetical subtitle continues for another 100 words or so, tucking in a variety of further references, and, in plain English, states that de la Mare's book was first prepared as a lecture, then edited and increased and enriched by borrowing from various other texts, and finally made into the book before us. In stating so much, it provides an elegant small play upon this antique convention—complete with sustained, nearly exhausted, metaphor—which all students of eighteenth century literature recognize and rejoice in.

When I first read it, de la Mare's playfulness reminded me of my own, years ago, when I had indiscreeted myself by sending to my editor a novel titled *Fabula Fabuli* , which in Latin means, "A Tale of a Bean." This was pretentious of me, and slyly dishonest, because I am not a competent

Latinist. I am hardly even an incompetent one. But the title was so neat and saucy, that I couldn't resist it; I thought it suited the novel with rare precision, since the novel itself was intended to be a crackling and defiant *scherzo*. It is also a first-person narrative told by a woefully miscast produce warehouse worker named Asa Bean—a young intellectual ironist who has dropped out of graduate school with the sure instinct of seeking out the limits of his own irrelevance.

But the pleasure given by that whimsically learned title was ephemeral. My editor, Hiram Haydn, phoned within a few weeks to inform me that when the people in Marketing (those tyrannous troglodytes who dominate publishing today, convinced they know more than editors because they are businesslike, rather than "literary") . . . . when these people saw the title, they were dismayed.

"There is no way," Hiram quoted them as saying, "that we can sell a novel with a title in Latin."

But I protested that the title was almost too delicious to resist, and Hiram half-agreed; but then asked if I wouldn't try to come up with a new title, anyway, and perhaps add a playful flourish or two, signifying why it had had to be changed. He was suggesting a compromise where I could sort of have my cake and eat it too.

It seems to me that Hiram Haydn's essential liberality and magnanimity are manifest in this episode. Certainly I was immediately aware of what a grand opportunity it was; given the context, it was almost better than the original would have been had it remained unchallenged and untroubled. So I seized joyously upon changing the title . . . which, in retrospect and in view of the novel's woefully exiguous sales (it was given a handsome, full-page review in *The New York Times Book Review* five months after publication, which did it no good, for by that time most bookstores had already returned their unsold copies), I now take special pleasure in quoting entirely, as follows:

> *The Tale of*
> **ASA BEAN**
> Originally Titled *Fabula Fabuli*,
> But Changed after Admonishment and
> Correction of the Author by the Publisher,

as having chosen a Title of too Great an
Irrelevancy to that Public Whose Imprimatur
is Deemed Essential to Literary Excellence,
and which title Signifies a tale about
one Asa Bean (himself Irrelevant according
to the Many), whose Wit (*ingenium*) is
Unnaturally High, whereas his Judgment
(*judicium*) is Naturally Low, and whose Story
is Accordingly Found to be a Human one.

I wonder how the Marketing people would have responded if this had
been the first title proffered. Would they have been equally dismayed?
Might they not have asked that I simply give the damned thing a Latin
title and be done with it? Is it possible they would have been right, and if
the novel had been published as *Fabula Fabuli*, it would have sold untold
numbers of copies, perhaps even as many as thirty or forty?

But please note that, like de la Mare, in my subtitle I have followed the
antique custom of capitalizing the first letters of Abstract Words, which
is to say, Words of Rhetorical Plangency, Substance, and Dignity; and
have enjoyed sketching out a mini-essay explaining things I would like to
be understood about the book, even though I naturally think that, for the
attentive and sympathetic reader, they are sufficiently evident in the text
itself.

❦   My present essay, however, is not about *The Tale of Asa
Bean;* nor is it about title pages; and it is not principally or literally about
desert islands. Initial signs notwithstanding, it is not headed in any of
those directions. It is not even about the designs provided for the text of
de la Mare's book by Rex Whistler—which are a bit too exquisite, for my
taste, with the frontispiece showing an unnecessarily epicene Indian sitting
atop a symbolic islet. (I prefer F. Rowland Emett's illustrations for de la
Mare's *Peacock Pie, A Book of Rhymes*, London, 1941.)

But illustrations, good or bad, are also beside the point, for my subject
is the imagination in the act of isolating itself. Here is a theme that Asa

Bean understood fabulously well, and spent his hours and days document-
ing to his own full satisfaction, if not to the satisfaction of certain anonymous marketing executives, not to mention all those millions of readers
who know nothing whatsoever about the by-now fabulous "A. Bean."

My turning away from de la Mare's work, however, should not suggest
that it is unworthy of direct and extended treatment. *Desert Islands* is a
curious and interesting book. It is, to the best of my knowledge, unique;
for of the 305 pages that constitute *Desert Islands* , the main text consists
of only seventy-two, while the remaining 224 are devoted to footnotes,
followed by nine pages of Acknowledgments and Index.

I know of no other book whose footnotes outnumber the text by more
than three-to-one. And yet, in one way, such a seeming disproportion is
indicative of a most printworthy text, for the secret of every text is innerness
and implication, and footnotes reveal something of this innerness and
literally spell out that which would otherwise remain implicit . . . somewhat
in the way of old-fashioned title pages, now that I think of it—for what is
a garrulous subtitle if not the title page's version of a footnote?

Still, to repeat, it is not de la Mare's book I am writing about. The text
for my present excursion might seem almost incidental. It is provided on
the verso of the page from which I quoted at the beginning. On this page,
de la Mare explains what *his* purpose is, and what it is not: "The enterprise
is at least the reverse of anything truly critical. Against that, let Mr. Ralph
Hodgson's sovereign plea be my defence:

> Reason has moons, but moons not hers
> Lie mirror'd on her sea
> Confounding her astronomers,
> But, O! delighting me.

Upon first reading this, I felt a shock that was almost physical. Upon
that first encounter, I could not, nor can I even now, at this moment, think
of more beautiful lines of poetry anywhere. When I first read the quatrain,
I reread it, again and again, hardly able to hear it often enough, and
yearning to explore all the intricate magic that looms within this tiny grid
of words. I yearned to talk about it, and study its images and intricacy of
idea. I yearned to think about it and wonder aloud . . . all of which is to
say, I wanted to teach it.

🐝   Although the quatrain itself was not only unexpected, but unfamiliar to me, I was not at all unacquainted with Ralph Hodgson. His work was once briefly known and even admired. However, today, if his name is mentioned at all, he is usually classified as one of the "minor lyricists" of the early twentieth century, and then conveniently dismissed. He did not, for example, write anything as obviously teachable, notable, or foot-notable as *The Waste Land* or *Harmonium*.

But he is a wonderful poet, at his best—and at what other level should a poet be judged? The verse I have quoted above supports and documents a judgment of his great merit; it also reveals that Hodgson's poetry is unlike any other. I first read his poem "Eve" sometime in the early 1960's, and remember feeling a sense of wonder in learning that Hodgson was not only still living, but living on a small farm in Ohio. His mailing address was given as "Minerva," which is somewhere near Akron. (I thought surely it had long since been swallowed up by some ravenous municipality, digested, and excreted as a shopping center; but I understand that it has not been, so maybe there is hope for the world.)

Minerva is a wonderfully apt name for a poet's village; but this is Minerva, *Ohio*—a place where poets are not supposed to live. Certainly, they are not supposed to live here by choice. Furthermore, Hodgson should have known better, for he was not just another provincial with a John Deere cap, a pack of Mail Pouch in his shirt pocket, and two speakers for his pickup. He was, in fact, an Englishman—an *Edwardian* Englishman—and you can't get any more English than that; furthermore, he had known something of the real world, having worked (as *Contemporary Authors*, Vol. 102, states) "as a journalist, draftsman, artist, publisher, and breeder of bull terriers." He also taught English Literature for a while in Japan.

What was a man like this doing in Minerva, Ohio? How did he get here, and why? His wife (evidently they had no children) was said to be a missionary and a teacher; was she originally from northeastern Ohio? Or had she been sent there from some civilized parish in order to convert the local heathen?

These were some of the questions I asked myself, and they seemed to me natural questions; but I hardly knew how to answer them, for Ralph Hodgson was that rarity among poets—one who not only claimed to be solitary, but actually maintained his remoteness from the public in a most uncompromising manner. (It is the consensus of even the gabbiest poets that writing is a lonely job; but most have their eye on a public forum, and few come anywhere near living up to their profession.) The information available from the most obvious sources about Hodgson is sketchy, impersonal, and highly redundant.

But the redundancy itself carries a certain authority. Information that is reprinted often enough and generally acknowledged to be true may turn out to be true, after all. Thus, when it is stated that Hodgson was born on March 12, 1871, in Northumberland, Yorkshire, and died in Minerva, Ohio, on November 3, 1962, I believe it. Such data are pale and innocuous, however, and I don't think even Hodgson would have resented their being generally known.

His published work is so scanty that Conrad Aiken referred to him as "a poet of very small production and of a production on a uniformly high level." I feel fortunate, in a way, for having "discovered him" for myself, so long ago; but I regret not writing to him, and perhaps—since we were both, at that time, Ohioans—even visiting him and risking a violation of his sacred privacy. But maybe that is just the bumptious midwestern American in me, for we native Ohioans assume that any normal, healthy, well-adjusted solitary poet would welcome a visitor anytime.

Evidently, some other writer must have visited him there, however, for *Time Magazine* reported that Hodgson was living "in near seclusion in a farmhouse near Minerva, Ohio." The poet's love for nature was as profound as his love for solitude, and his stated reason for moving to Ohio was that the birds here seemed to be just as interesting as in England. But, as if taking further thought, he added, " . . . and I'd never seen a hummingbird. It took my mind."

It took my mind. Probably his conversation was as laconic as his poetry; and both suggest depths of connection that leave us wondering. When he died in Minerva at the age of 91, Hodgson had, as *Time* stated, enjoyed "a long life of deeper privacy than most poets ever dream of." But even more significant is the following observation: "Hodgson shuns brilliant images that grasp the eye. His life is the same way. Passersby are shocked at the disrepair of the farm that he has never worked . . . . His real work is [to] wonder about the energy of anything that grows, moves, breathes, or flies: 'I don't try to reconcile anything. It's a damned strange world.' "

❦   On March 29, 1966, I ordered a copy of the first edition of Hodgson's poem, *Eve and Other Poems,* from Blackwells. This had been published as a small pamphlet for sixpence (I had to pay somewhat more) by a small press, "The Sign of the Flying Fame," in London in 1913. Hodgson himself was a partner in this small firm; and another partner was Holbrook Jackson, known by bibliophiles everywhere.

No one who has ever read "Eve" can forget the magical surge of its rhythms. At the risk of being repetitive, I will say that there is simply nothing else like it in English verse. It is too long to quote entire, but the first stanza gives some hint of its uncanny music:

> Eve, with her basket, was
> Deep in the bells and grass,
> Wading in bells and grass
> Up to her knees,
> Picking a dish of sweet
> Berries and plums to eat,
> Down in the bells and grass
> Under the trees.

I quote this uneasily, for two reasons: to the modern ear, generally distrustful of closed forms, such short lines of highly stressed dactyls and tight rhymes are too easily dismissed as doggerel; also, its effect is cumulative, and needs three or more stanzas to achieve its incantatory power . . . and, connected with this, I cannot be sure of how much of the verse's magic derives from my sense of knowing what follows, and how much is already there, in the first verse, audible for all who can hear and will take the time to listen.

The first charge will admit of no defense, and can be judged only by the ear. The second and third assume a privileged sense of the poem— one which I can claim simply by virtue of having read it several times in its entirety. But lest I sound too smug and proprietary in stating this, as if I knew Hodgson's work well, let me make an embarrassing confession: while I had possessed this little chapbook for over twenty years—I had not, in all that time, read beyond the title poem . . . although I had read "Time, You Old Gypsy Man," which precedes it, finding it good and interesting, though inescapably quaint.

But for some reason, through all these years of owning the pamphlet and having it on my shelf, I had never read the three small poems at the end. And this only serves me right, for there is a crude sort of poetic justice in the fact that the very last of those three poems that end the chapbook is . . . you guessed it: a quatrain whose first line is: "Reason has moons, but moons not hers . . . ." And to think that this small, dense miracle was there all the time, and I had no knowledge of the fact, nor of what this fact might mean.

Perhaps, if you believe in signs (and I do—with reservations, of course), you might think of this as a sign that it was somehow not meant for me, as a brash younger man, to go visit the old poet, after all. But now, through the intermediation of Walter de la Mare and his book, *Desert Islands*, I have visited Hodgson at last, better prepared for the visit by over two decades, and visiting him precisely where it is probable he believed he most truly lived—not in the Yorkshire of his birth, nor even in Minerva, Ohio; but in the words and rhythms of a most beautiful, suggestive, and remarkable lyric.

It is a damned strange world, indeed.

❦   Naturally curious about Hodgson, I thought of my friend, Dean Keller, of the Kent State University Library. This man is a bibliophile who is not only knowledgeable in modern literature, generally, but knows Hodgson's work well; furthermore, he lives within, say, a robin's flight of Minerva.

So I wrote to him, and in his return letter, Dean told me about Hodgson's book, *Poets Remembered*, Cleveland (1967), a title I was as ignorant of as a squirrel is of metaphysics. Of course I was interested, so Dean loaned me his copy, shipping it by mail, so that I might possibly learn a little more about the mysterious Hodgson.

When I opened the package, I found a slender handsome book with a green dust jacket over pale green and gray binding, with the endsheets and paste-downs covered with Hodgson's drawings of famous literary figures and their connections with dogs. There was Virginia Woolf's Flush and Blake's "Dog starved at his master's gate"—both of which I knew about; but I had not known that Matthew Arnold had written two elegies for dogs, nor did I know that Sir Walter Scott "discovered the Dandie Dinmont Terrier, and gave the breed its name."

This handsome publication was the 75th Anniversary offering of that distinguished group of bibliophiles, The Rowfant Club of Cleveland (like so many places, it turns out, not far from Minerva). The title piece was printed from the text of a public address given at Eastern Michigan University in 1943. It is light, chatty, and full of references to Hodgson's association among the British *literati* near the turn of the century. But there is little in it that would cause one to think that its author might have written anything more than an acceptable poem.

Following this piece, are "Ten of the Poems for Which [Hodgson] Is Respected" (our quatrain is not among them); and then, following these, and ending the book, is a short biographical note by Robert James Izant, that begins as follows: "On November 3, 1962 death came to Ralph Hodgson, renowned English poet, at age ninety-one in a sequestered spot in rural Ohio where he and his wife had made their home for a score of years."

This rather ponderous opening does not lead to startling revelations; although it does reveal something that justifies it in its entirety, and perhaps helps explain the secret affinity I felt in that quatrain: *Hodgson was a collector of rare books.* It also solves the mystery of his coming to Minerva, for it tells us that in Japan, Hodgson met Aurelia Bolliger, of Canton, Ohio (alas, near Minerva); and it may be inferred that it was due to her influence that the poet eventually came to Ohio to live, where there are hummingbirds to take the minds of those who have minds for the taking.

In this book there are also photographs of Hodgson, including one with his wife—a woman smiling out of a pleasantly round face. In all the photos he appears as a dishevelled, bewhiskered, pipe-smoking old man. And, in all but one, he is also smiling, as genial-looking as any old extroverted ham before a camera; but in that exception, he sits bemused, looking off camera to the side, with his spectacles pulled up over his forehead, like an old-time aviator's goggles as he gazes out of his cockpit into the wind drift. On the floor before him is a galvanized bucket, and the room does not appear to be too inhibited by neatness. Nevertheless, in still another photo, their white farm house is shown; and, from a distance, it looks very tidy, in spite of what *Time Magazine* said.

Hodgson's own poems in *Poets Remembered* are, with perhaps one exception, as crafted and elegant as one would expect. However, in my view, there is nothing that quite reaches the utter perfection of the quatrain quoted at the beginning of this piece.

But there is one poem that is an utter astonishment. It attracted me particularly, for it is titled "My Books," and it has two of the strangest, wackiest stanzas I have ever read, in or out of poetry:

> Volumes gay and volumes grave,
> Many volumes have I got;
> Many volumes though I have,
> Many volumes have I not.

> I have not the rare Lucasta,
> London, 1649:
> I'm a lean-pursed poetaster
> Or the book had long been mine.

Well, this is hilarious stuff; and to treat it solemnly would be to miss a delicious bit of humor. For one thing, when Lucasta is pronounced *Lucaster*, it rhymes with "disaster"; and there is no reason to pretend that it doesn't. The English have a wonderful gift for mispronouncing the obvious, it is true: the Elizabethan epigrammatist, Thomas Bastard pronounced his last name to rhyme with "petard"; Phyllis Bottome rhymed her surname with "Madame" (as the French say it); and Oliver Onions rhymed his with "O'Brien's"; but nobody's fooled by such subtleties. And Lucy Sacheverell—who no doubt pronounced her name "Chevrolet" and was supposed to have been Richard Lovelace's inspiration for Lucasta—would surely have done a few turns in her grave if she could have heard that one.

Still, the poem doesn't end nearly so wackily, and I simply don't know what to make of it. An adequate analogy eludes me; however, the poem—far too long to quote here, and I wouldn't know what to do with it if I did quote it entire—starts out somewhat like a polka rendered by Borah Minnevich and the Harmonica Rascals and ends like a lost or discarded passage from the score of *Fidelio*.

With that analogy, I have drifted far enough; I had better return to my theme of desert islands, which—if Fate is kind—we will not have left so far behind that we will never find them again, so that they will be deserted forever, and beyond all conception. Such will not be the case, if they are the right sort of desert islands.

❦ Walter de la Mare's purpose in writing his book was to explore the uncanny appeal that desert islands have for most of us. It isn't simply DeFoe's masterpiece he was talking about; he was talking about desert islands as symbolic places, mythic and unforgettable in the mind.

In truth, the subject extends beyond literary artifacts. Having mentioned *Robinson Crusoe, The Tempest,* and *The Swiss Family Robinson* we descend to images of the popular mind: think of all those cartoons showing a man on a desert island the size of a dining room table, with a single palm tree growing out of it—an emblem of human helplessness and loneliness that occupies a strange place in our imaginations, and exercises a strange power, for such islands do not literally exist.

Then there are all of those jokes about desert islands, along with those once-popular hypotheses, such as: "If you were stranded on a desert island, what ten books would you choose to have with you?" The equivalent today would probably be videotapes, or maybe computers; assuming the island is equipped with electricity and back-up equipment. And now, the notion extends even to doctors and a brand of aspirin—or some aspirin substitute—if I actually heard and saw what I think I heard and saw on the television recently. The question was, "What pain remedy would 1000 doctors choose if they were stranded on a desert island?"

No man is an island, certainly; but we all have them inside, and they are as deserted and lonely as Crusoe's. Joseph Conrad's great novel, *Victory* has as its protagonist a man named Axel Heyst, who lives all alone on an island in what were then (*Victory* was published in 1915) the Dutch East Indies. Heyst is a philosopher who has renounced the world and its madness; but his private little Eden is eventually penetrated by a lovely young woman, named Lena, along with three melodramatic desperadoes. Being human, they are nothing less than the world come to visit; and eventually they in one way or other destroy Axel Heyst, so that the victory of the title must necessarily be the victory of life, fate, or possibly simply the world of human contact, over any conceivable strategy to escape it.

Conrad's Heyst is doomed, partly because he is so idealistic (indeed, it is because of the intransigency of his idealism that he has tried to escape the world); thus, he is a genuine tragic hero, and one of great power and conviction. But the relevant point here is that he has sought out a desert island—that ultimate image of remoteness—as his haven.

This decision was a radical one, and we are meant to understand that, while he was in most ways a good man, his failure is fore-ordained; there is no escaping the world, and to go to such extremes suggests a personality that borders upon the pathological.

Nevertheless, just as the desert islands de la Mare writes about are mostly in the imagination (and as Heyst's island was for Conrad, if not for Heyst himself, who was confined to the world of the text) . . . just as desert islands are not literally to be sought out when the world is too much with us, so can we find desert islands within ourselves, if we search hard enough, and know how to look.

There are, in truth, many sorts of desert islands for us to inhabit. Years ago, I planned to write a short story about a man who craved privacy so much he wanted to advertise the fact. I pictured this fellow as an average sort, except for this one notion that troubled him. He had read somewhere that Howard Hughes (then still alive) had everything in the world he wanted except for the one thing that most of us have without seeking, but had become for him more precious than all his wealth: privacy. Thinking of this, my private hero broods upon his own personal possession of this gift that has been denied to one who was perhaps, at that time, the wealthiest man in the world; but he doesn't know what to do with it.

The story has not been written, partly because I didn't know any more what to do with *it* than my hero did with his own privacy. (And what can be more private than an unexpressed story idea?) I still think the idea is a good one. I viewed my protagonist as a sort of Everyman, and thought that his story could be a deep and interesting one, if I could get it exactly right. But now that I've written about it here, I probably won't have to write it as a story; so maybe it's fitting that it has found itself in this present account . . . as if all this time it has been headed for *this* eventuation, rather than the story I thought I would write.

But the idea is larger than any story; it has to do with islands of every conceivable sort. I am thinking of metaphorical islands—the islands of the mind, the islands of unread texts—many of them uncharted territories, so far as living readers are concerned; I am thinking of real places where one can go to find the imagination alone with itself.

I am thinking of the least likely places for a poet to live, away from publishers, editors, critics, and all who might be said to constitute the poetic establishment. I am thinking of Minerva, Ohio—a place I have still never actually visited, so far as I know (although I must have passed by it many times); but where there was once a very old man who lived with his wife in midwestern rural seclusion . . . a man who loved solitude, rare books, poetry, birds, and bull terriers.

And I am thinking of his reason for going there—"reason" in both senses of the word, having to do with both logic and purpose. Reason is far more mysterious than most people think, and logicians are increasingly troubled by it, for it reflects realities that cannot be seen in themselves. Ralph Hodgson understood this, and long before he had ever seen Minerva, Ohio, he had written that magic poem that begins, "Reason has moons, but moons not hers . . . ."

And yet, even as he wrote it, there was a private place waiting for him— a sort of island in the future, surrounded by time and the world's ignorance; an island that was remote and far from the imaginings of those who considered themselves most civilized, most sophisticated, most knowledgeable; an island which he eventually journeyed to, and lived there for many years before he died, keeping this part of "a damned strange world" all to himself and reading and collecting books and watching birds, and writing hardly anything more, if indeed he wrote anything at all.

So far as I know, he didn't write anything else in all those years he lived in Minerva; and this is strange, in a way. Even in cartoons, stranded mariners put messages in bottles and throw them into the ocean, with the hope that somebody, somewhere, will find and read them.

And as one who has written and had published a considerable number of poems, I can vouch for the fact that having a poem published in these days is not entirely unlike writing that other sort of message and putting it in a bottle and throwing it into an indifferent surf. What little chance there is that it will be received as intended, or that the finder will be able to conceive of where it is you really live! Still, it is one of the world's little, though ultimately immeasurable, sadnesses to contemplate the fact that Ralph Hodgson did not send any messages forth from that unlikely island of solitude called Minerva, Ohio.

Whatever messages he might have sent, I like to think, would have been short and to the point. They would have been just the sort of laconic rune to stuff into an old bottle. But those messages, like all the best ones, would have been pointed in a way that no one before had ever guessed . . . crying out for directions that none of the rest of us stranded mariners had ever thought of before, with a hope that there might be those who could read it in ways that not even the language, itself—in all its commodious tolerance—could ever have precisely anticipated.

For that is what a poem does; and, like Reason, all her astronomers are confounded, because more is reflected than can ever be seen in that other, larger, more obvious world.

POSTSCRIPT

I have since learned that Hodgson did not entirely cease publishing after settling in Minerva. In 1941 and 1942, two chapbooks, "Silver Wedding" and "The Muse and the Mastiff" were printed by the Boerner Printing Company "for the author." It would seem that Hodgson subsidized them. That a poet of his achievement should resort to vanity publishing is dismaying—although he would not have been the first writer of ability to be forced to such a desperate extreme.

Furthermore, I have finally visited Minerva, Ohio, and am happy to report that it is a beautiful village situated deep in wooded hills—one that does not seem in the least danger of being swallowed up by urban gluttony. It's no wonder Hodgson chose to live here.

Also, in view of one Minerva woman's acrimonious response to "Hodgson's Island" when it appeared in *The Ohio Magazine*, I should explain my satiric references to the tobacco-chewing farmer and to Hodgson's wife having been sent to "convert the local heathen"; these were meant to satirize—not Ohioans, but those who hold such views of us. I am a fourth generation Ohioan and proud of the fact.

Such a misunderstanding is enough to make me foreswear irony forever; and I would do so if I had the character to make the vow stick.

❦ *Turmoil, Confusion, and Civil War Newspapers*

In reading the statistics of men killed in past wars, we are not likely to be perplexed or astounded. We know, for example, that a small, but relatively sizable, number of soldiers died in the Revolution; and that the number of fatalities in the Civil War was vast, almost beyond counting. Even though we may not have the precise numbers at our fingertips, as we say, we are nevertheless in the presence of essentially familiar knowledge when we encounter such facts.

And yet, statistics are the barest of abstractions, and we are always a little surprised when we are confronted with carnal evidence of how much tumult and wrath lay behind those old body counts. We find it odd that there were actually contemporary issues which aroused the passions of great teeming populations. Who, having read about the Missouri Compromise for a history course, could have guessed? But there it is: we are naively astonished when forced to realize that people back in all those troubled times of warfare didn't just kill one another; by golly, they were *mad!*

In truth, it is a shame that war can't remain a matter of strategy, bolstered by statistics. Come to think of it, maybe for some of those in the Pentagon, this is pretty much what it is. No doubt we'd all be happier if military action existed only as an abstraction, in those forms of distancing that statistics, along with officialese and euphemisms, provide. I imagine that for all but a pathological few, warfare is best enjoyed from a great distance. I say this as something of an authority, for as a boy I loved to play with toy soldiers. Certainly, warfare is radically different as viewed strategically, from without, from what it is in the turmoil and confusion of the midst— as experienced, for example, by those poor befuddled soldier boys portrayed in *The Red Badge of Courage.*

For most of us, most of the time, the Civil War exists either as a vague historical fact looming somewhere just over the horizon of our consciousness, awaiting some call for citation or of relevance . . . or, it is some cluster of data more or less available for recall (e.g., "The Battle of Bull Run was fought on July 21, 1861, and was the only major engagement of that year.")

While there have been few events in the history of mankind that have been so thoroughly documented as the Civil War, much of what has been written is textbook history, which is to say, abstract and general, giving little real sense of the violent passions and confusions of those extraordinary years. Such historical treatises are necessary for understanding the structure of events, of course; but in concentrating upon the paradigms, one loses all feel for their human density. You can't see the trees for the forest, in a manner of speaking.

For example, consider the following data. When Confederate General John Morgan crossed the Ohio river into Union territory, he brought 2,640 men with him. Then, by the end of his bold foray, the damages to property in the State of Ohio alone (not counting the costs of financing the Militia) amounted to $576,225. Here we have facts that bracket, chronologically, what has become known as "Morgan's Raid"; but where is the sense of life as we know it? Were the people who provided such statistics actually real living people who could suffer from poison ivy and head colds, not to mention greed, loneliness, envy, ignorance, and spite?

Contrast those facts cited above, with the following passage from a Civil War Regimental History:

> The troops advanced slowly toward the Sharpsburg and Hagerstown Turnpike. We passed over open fields and through orchards and gardens, and the men filled their pockets and empty haversacks with apples. About dusk sharp musketry and cannonading began in our front. It was nine o'clock at night when our brigade reached the position assigned it. The men laid [sic] down upon the ground, formed in close column, muskets loaded and lines parallel with the turnpike. Once or twice during the night, heavy volleys of musketry crashed in the dark woods on our left. There was a drizzling rain, and with the certain prospect of deadly conflict on the morrow, the night was dismal.[1]

1. Dawes, Rufus R. *Service with the Sixth Wisconsin Volunteers*, Marietta, Ohio., 1890. p. 87. The "deadly conflict on the morrow" was the Battle of Antietam.

When I read such a passage as this, I can well understand why there are so many enthusiastic collectors of Civil War regimental histories. In a modest way, and peripherally, I also collect them; but I have only a half dozen or so (mostly Ohio regiments), which is scarcely a good start. Therefore, I envy those who are sufficiently active, accomplished, and knowledgeable to collect "regimentals." And, in this context, at least, it seems to me that envy is good for the soul, for I respect and admire such collectors, rejoice in the sharp focus of their endeavors, and do not in the least begrudge them their good fortune and good taste.

Much of the interest of Civil War regimentals lies in their personal witnessing, their richness of human detail (those hungry soldier boys pausing to stuff apples in their gear), their function as autobiography. Those who wrote them relied upon three sources: personal memory; the oral testimony of others; and public documentation, in the form of logs, journals, newspaper reports, and later published accounts of various campaigns. It is in the nature of such things that all of these sources tended to flow together in the minds of the authors, so that when two or three wrote about the same regiments in the same campaigns, their perspectives—formed from different accounts, sense of proportion, and narrative instincts—could provide interestingly different versions.

These regimental histories are wonderful books. I have never read a dull one. Furthermore, the War of the Rebellion was such good material, that even those ponderous, once-popular, nineteenth-century autobiographies of ministers and statesmen—which can be as lifeless as flint or clay—will often, if there is a section devoted to some personal participation in the Civil War, come suddenly alive in miraculous ways. Hemingway wrote that war is the only subject for a writer. He was wrong in this; but demonstrably and beyond doubt it is a very great subject. Events that threaten life or death can have a marvelous effect upon one's ability to concentrate and gather impressions.

But for all their excellence, regimental histories are limited in obvious ways. Many were written so long after the fact, that their accounts had been altered by memory's unconscious revisions, along with more conscious editing. Naturally, their long historical perspective allows for certain sorts of truth and judgment precisely as it excludes others. Nevertheless, they were necessarily historical and autobiographical, therefore, to some extent, self-conscious and rhetorical.

But where can one find more forthright, less self-conscious versions of what was happening—not just on the battlefields or in the halls of government, but in the heads of the people? In personal diaries and letters, to be sure. A few of these are excellent, and some of the best have been published. However, many of the diaries and letters in their natural state (i.e., unpublished) are so limited in their focus—or so perfunctory or illiterate—that they are of little use or interest.

Nevertheless, there is one fairly accessible resource that is in some ways nearly perfect for conveying a sense of the thoughts and feelings of the populace and the fullness of their time: I speak of contemporary newspapers—especially those newspapers nearest the scenes of battle. *Especially* especially, newspapers from the border states.

Most literary and historical texts are to some extent subtly shaped, if not warped and ruined, by a certain inevitable rhetoric. And in order to achieve a legitimate and necessary long-range perspective, they assume the posture of lecturing (even as I am doing this very moment). There's nothing wrong with such didacticism, of course; it is perfectly valid, for we all understand the worthiness of a well-prepared and well-reasoned speech or essay.

But newspapers provide a different sort of witnessing; they are too pragmatic, too caught up in quotidian strife, too intent upon reporting the latest events to be much bothered by long-range impressions. Of course they are not devoid of rhetoric; but their rhetoric is itself of the moment, part of the speech and tone of the era, and therefore testimonial. It is precisely their limitations as journalism, their narrowly practical function as things of the moment, that give them unique value.

Thus it is that in reading formal histories, we are part of an audience being lectured to by someone; but in reading old newspapers, we are eavesdropping, listening to dead people as they talk to one another, as they report on the latest news, rumor, and gossip, and strive to convince or confound living antagonists rather than impress future generations.

And the best part of it is, they don't even know we're listening.

❦   Last week, as I write this, I came upon five copies of *The Nashville Daily Union* and one of *The Louisville Daily Journal* in a country antique shop, and added them to a stack of ten or twelve books I was buying. The earliest of these newspapers was published on April 12, 1863, and the last, February 25, 1865. These first and last dated copies were Nashville papers, of different sizes (the largest is 5 ½ inches wider than our modern newspaper, and 4 inches longer) and filled with all sorts of fascinating information. The ads themselves are worth a year's subscription.

Consider the Sept. 9, 1863 issue of *The Nashville Daily Union*, whose ads offer soldier's pocket albums (for photographs of girlfriends or mothers), medicines to treat "diseases of a private nature" ("Gonorrhea cured without nauseous medicines or interference with business"—business ?), gold pens, lamps, watches, hats, boots, "mourning goods" (featuring English and French bombazines, black silks, and English crepes), rye whiskey, catawba and claret wines, "fine old Otard brandy, 1840," cigars, dry goods, jewelry, books, a buggy, "an elegant pianoforte," gas and steam pipe, etc.

One of my favorite ads is that of the Quartermaster's Depot, offering for sale to the highest bidder, "the following steamboats, wrecked in the Cumberland river, with Machinery, and other appurtenances, as they lay in the river." These vessels are the steamer "W.R. Sidell, near the head of Harpeth Shoals" and the steamer "Charter, five miles above Harpeth Shoals." I only wish I knew how much these two riverboats brought . . . and I wish I could have been there, because they sound like the sorts of things I tend to bid on. But barring that, I would have liked to be there afterwards, simply to see how the successful bidders went about pumping their riverboats out and getting them to float again.

Real estate was not neglected, even in those wildly unstable times. "Two beautiful blocks of lots" are offered in a no-nonsense ad that is headed, FOR A RICH MAN. Though prices are not given, several of the real estate ads specify payment in "Union Bank money," suggesting that the rich buyer referred to probably had to be not just any sort of rich buyer, but one who was rich in the right currency, according to the latest predictions.

Another ad announces that the boat bridge over the Cumberland River is open for travel. Directly above this, still another cries out: "500 Wood Choppers Wanted" while, to the right, Dr. M'Gill, Botanic Physician, offers to treat, among other conditions, "Affection of the lungs, Diseases of the throat, Dropsy, Swelled joints [sic], Stiff Limbs, Pleurisy . . . ." etc.

No private diseases are mentioned in either of these ads, which, of course, allows them to remain private.

Then there is an ad for the Chegaray Institute, a "Boarding and Day School for Young Ladies" all the way back east, and north, in Philadelphia. We are told that, "The regular course of instruction embraces the English and French languages—Latin if required, and all the branches which constitute a thorough English education, especial attention being paid to the latter by the Principal, assisted by the best Professors." I find myself groping for what, specifically, the word "latter" refers to, and am forced to conclude that this sentence itself was translated from the French—an idea that is supported by the following statement that, "French is the language of the family, and is constantly spoken in the institute."

So much is comforting to know, in view of the problem the institute seems to be having with English. Still, the ad itself has a certain *spirituel* quality—as much as would be consistent with familial virtues, at least. These homey virtues are emphasized, and given a frankly valedictorian flourish, by the name that ends the ad, as if signing a personal letter: "Madame D'Hervilly, Principal."

🐛 Those sample ads from *The Nashville Daily Union* seem to me wonderfully informative. By now, you know the 1863 version of the Nashville sound. But I have promised turmoil and confusion, and it is only right that you should be served. For this purpose I will turn to the single issue of *The Louisville Daily Journal* which I purchased that day a week or so past. It is dated Wednesday, April 22, 1863. Like its Nashville cousin, it is not only larger, but made of far better quality paper than today's newspaper. In fact, its feel suggests a strong rag content.

The ads are pretty much like those in Nashville. Evidently, they had private diseases in Louisville, too . . . along with hog cholera, not to mention cures for same. But here there is a touch of elegance that one might find wanting in Nashville. For example, fresh Potomac shad was advertised as available in the St. Charles Restaurant as well as in the Walker Exchange. And the Kentucky Eating House advertised "warm meals at all hours at 25 cents per meal."

But even the menus of the St. Charles, the Walker Exchange, and the Kentucky Eating House together could not be as richly various as the offerings of the paper in which their advertisements appeared, for when you open these large sheets (all the papers I bought are simply great folios, without inner leaves), the world itself seems to open before your eyes.

Fancy? Well, let me demonstrate. Is it sidewalks you're after? Then note that the sidewalk on the north side of Main, "from the west line of Mr. Hanna's property to Fourth Street" shall be paved. And who is it that cries out for news about hogs? Directly beneath the above, there appears, "NOTICE TO OWNERS OF HOGS," which notifies them that the ordinance against their running loose in the streets ("except butchers' and those for slaughtering purposes") will be enforced, and the fine is "$5 for each and every day."

Only one column leftward is a List of deceased soldiers who have died in hospitals at St. Louis, from April 9, to 16, 1863. The dead are identified by name and regiment alone (most regiments are midwestern, with one rather odd exception, "John H. Hudson, co. C., 4th Virginia." The list is twenty names long; and as a student of onomastics, I notice that all but "Metz" and "Kelly" are WASP names, as surely as if they had been cast by Hollywood in 1938.

Such homogeneity notwithstanding, what contrasts and paradoxes these great wide pages hold! The left column of the first page is a listing of bulletins, indicated literally by indexes, which is to say, images of hands with index fingers pointing to the right. One of these (which is unaccountably missing its index) announces the "large and talented troop" of Sharpley's Minstrels. They must have been famous, for it is said of them: "In the comic element they stand pre-eminent."

Directly beneath, there are announcements concerning the delay of a Nashville train, the arrest of a man selling bogus discharge papers, and the arrival of 500 soldiers in town to procure horses for the troops to the south. Of these, it is reported, "A number of them 'indulged too freely' after they arrived, and this morning we observed the guards picking them up promiscuously."

Nearby, for the sake of variety, there is the report of a panther, "measuring seven feet from nose to tip of tail [which] was killed within five and a half miles of Lexington, Ky., on the old Frankfort road."

And then, under the headline, DEATH BY POISON, there is an account of a Mrs. Murphy who walked to the city, "and on her return home she felt unwell, and supposing she had a chill took some powders which she thought was quinine. It proved to be some sort of rat poison, and in fifteen minutes she was a corpse."

All I have quoted from this single issue of the *Louisville Daily Journal,* from the shad ads of the St. Charles and Walker's Exchange clear down to poor Mrs. Murphy (who probably couldn't read, so why did she want to stay alive, anyway?) . . . all of this appears on the first page, before we've hardly gotten started, and—while we've mentioned hogs running loose—we haven't yet mentioned the cure for Hog Cholera ("The Great Remedy of the Age") or the ad for men to enlist in the 365th Kentucky Mounted Infantry, or Dr. La Croix's "Private Medical Treatise on the Physiological View of Marriage" or Tarrant's Effervescent Seltzer Aperient, or the ad that reads, "Confidential, Young Men Who Have Injured themselves by certain secret habits, which unfit them for business, pleasure or the duties of married life; also, middle-aged men and old men, who from the follies of youth or other causes, feel a debility in advance of their years, before placing themselves under the treatment of any one, should first read, 'The Secret Friend.' "

What was that last? Yes, you are right: it might have been written by Madame D'Hervilly herself, although it probably was not; still, the possibility that it was penned by one of her alumnae is not altogether unthinkable.

But the point is, these addenda have themselves appeared in only one column, still on the first page! And we have skipped over five columns (these noble sheets contain eight columns, requiring long arms and steady nerves from readers in those days), and have passed over large areas of interest (ads for Henry rifles, Ladies' dress goods, cigars, and military goods, including "presentation swords and sabres"), along with what one naturally associates with Kentuckiana, namely, a sale of thoroughbreds and "trotting stock," for June 17, 1863. These were "125 head of thorough-bred colts, and fillies of various ages," personally selected and advertised by B.A. Alexander, of Woodford County, Kentucky.

Then, directly above the above is an ad by Lieut. Peterson, of Lexington, who wishes "to recruit a number of stout, able-bodied men, Tennesseans, as Drivers, gunners, Smiths, Buglers, Saddlers, & c" for a battery of light artillery. To emphasize regional allegiance, he specifies that, "Persons who have friends in the Tennessee Regiments can be with them by enlisting in a Tennessee Battery, commanded by Tennessee officers."

Like the Daily Union, the Journal is vocal in its Unionist sympathy, although perhaps a shade less ardent, and (still on the first page) quotes a letter "taken from a dead rebel," after the Battle of Stone River. Referred to as "a specimen of curious orthography," the letter is quoted, beginning as follows: "Der Sun I reseve your letter on the 27 not on the 14 insent, this the 28, it found us all well. I hant Ben well and it levs us the same hopen that these few lines may find you in good health and property."

You get the idea. The letter is quoted entire, including the name of the poor illiterate Alabama soldier who wrote it. The editor's intent is clear, for the tone of the piece reveals the assumption of a sympathetic audience; thus, all who read it—probably even some of Madame D'Hervilly's pupils—were given the opportunity to enjoy themselves hugely and even feel superior for a moment, or however long it took them to read the letter.

🐝   Appearances notwithstanding, I have actually gotten around to turning the first page of *The Louisville Daily Journal.* I have scanned the second, third, and even the fourth pages. You should be forewarned, however, that I intend to return to the first page, for one additional flourish. However, it is a law of common sense, nature, and Euclidean proprieties that before coming back, one must necessarily go somewhere else.

But I will take you there in confidence, for it is my thesis that virtually everything in all of these newspapers is worthy of our attention; and if this is the case, it follows logically that the material beyond page one of the Journal should be attended to, however briefly.

So far, I have not dwelt upon military events, which may seem odd, for all the readers of these papers must have been hungry for every report from the various battle lines and campaigns that raged about them. The Nashville Union was filled with such news, and so is the Daily Journal. If the second page features an ad for the forthcoming "running races" of the Mound City Jockey Club, it also has room (left column) for military news.

The Battle of Ironclads in Charleston harbor is reported. "We had hardly a hope of success. We had a strong apprehension of defeat. And there has been a defeat." Such laconic prose embodies the message it is meant to convey. Its leaden spirit is hardly raised by the levity at the bottom of the page, stating that, "Jeff Davis has issued another address to his people. If not a man of address, he is a man of many addresses." This would be a poor joke even in a time of peace, but in the present circumstance, it is downright demoralizing, and hardly worth the index that points it out.

The most surprising military reference, from our perspective, is an editorial comment relating to the Federal troops gathered before Vicksburg: "Gen. Grant, for aught that appears, has long been to all intents and purposes motionless, and is so still. Even the canal work, from which so much was hoped, has come to a dead stop. In the mean while, the rebel authorities, having no apprehensions for Vicksburg, may quietly order one half or three fourths of their army to join Gen. Joe Johnston in Middle Tennessee, for an attack on Gen. Rosecrans or for an invasion of Kentucky." Who, knowing about the first bloody attack upon Vicksburg one month later—not to mention the subsequent progress of the war—could believe that Grant would ever have been accused of idleness and/or timidity?

The writing in the Journal is no better than the jokes; but it is informative, after all, for it conveys to us how things looked before there were those historical closures that now define them. Such editorial unease reveals the openness of events, the confusion and uncertainty, when there could have been no clear indication of how things would turn out, and what sort of leader Grant, for example, would prove to be.

Skipping rightwards past more ads (some asking to buy gold and Southern bank notes; others offering "Musketo Netting" and oysters and seeds and pistols for sale) . . . going clear to page three, left column, we come upon an astonishing editorial (indexed, like the bulletins), beginning, "Yesterday was extremely dull in everything pertaining to items of a local nature. A heavy rain set in at noon and continued without intermission up to the hour of going to press."

There is considerably more in the same key, before the editorial breaks off to leave room for announcement of the sale of Government bonds; then, below that, the availability of a handbook of tax law; then a report of a "rebel force which menaced Columbia, Adair county, the fore part of last week"; then a forthcoming "grand juvenile fancy dress ball"; then a statement that the "rebel accounts of the recent battle near Somerset are distinguished for falsehood."

There is also the report of an invasion "rolled back" by a Col. Hobson "in the direction of Monroe county," along with the report of counterfeit fifty cent postal notes, and the fact (noted at the bottom of the page) that "Oliver Lucas qualified yesterday as a Notary Public."

Well, the Lucas report doesn't excite me a great deal (in spite of the fact he may have proved to be a first-rate Notary); however, even though yesterday might have been extremely dull in "items of a local nature," there was sure a hell of a lot happening nearby. But then I may be too easily entertained, for I find even the following interesting: "Six prisoners, all females, escaped from the Covington jail on Friday night, by removing a few bricks from the west wall of the building. Four of them have been recaptured."

Maybe I'm just a patsy, when it comes to being interested. But I'll fight the tendency, going so far as to omit reference to The Great Indian Medicine called "The Cherokee Cure"; and I'll not pause over the silverware ads and the river news. But I do want to refer to the auction sales announced on page three. In one of these, "Linen, cotton, and silk handkerchiefs" are offered along with "Hosiery, Gloves, Laces, Hair Nets, Whips; together with a large line of notions." (*Whips?* I'll probably never know.)

This reference to auctions reminds me that it is time to go back to page one, for there is an auction listed there, too. In fact, it is, in a sense, where I have been headed all along; it is prominently placed, in the fourth column, two-thirds down the page. It is correctly labeled, "Sheriff's Sale," and occupies about five inches. But it is not like those on page three, for here there are no sprightly lists of consumer goods offered for sale to the highest bidder. There is, in fact, only one commodity listed: slaves. Twenty of them are offered for sale. The great majority are men, along with two or three women and two or three boys. (One name, "Jewell," listed as weighing 100 pounds, could be a boy or girl or woman.)

I confess that I was surprised by this. I found it incongruous in a newspaper of manifest Union sympathy. But then I remembered what is so easily forgotten: that the Civil War was fought primarily to preserve the union, not to free the slaves. I should not have been surprised at all, for I knew that there were active unionists who did not necessarily find slavery an evil. Or, if they did find it an evil, it was not one of such magnitude as to justify going to war.

And yet, previous knowledge notwithstanding, this remains puzzling. I promised turmoil and confusion, and I believe we have found them here, in this announcement. The simple fact that great numbers of people believe something to be true does not make it true; it doesn't even make it plausible. I'm sure that most of the 1863 populace of Louisville found nothing at all inconsistent in their advocacy for the Union *uber alles*, and the comfortable old institution of slavery.

But if one remembers this, it is important not to be guilty of a temporal sort of ethnocentrism ("chronocentrism," perhaps). Before we apply our current standards of morality and decency upon the Past, we should try to understand it, as nearly as possible, for what it was in itself—not what it would be judged as being if it existed today, among people much like ourselves. "The times change, and we change with them," the old Latin proverb states; and as "we" change, so do our standards of justice, even though the law is a conservative institution, dedicated to the principle of continuity in itself and all other institutions.

This is to say, for all its limitations as an institution (not to mention its horrors), slavery was not an isolated viciousness. It was part of a world that, like ours, possessed its own odd integrity. In thinking of slavery, it should be remembered that, by today's standards, a general brutality pervaded all human relationships in those times. Why else was there all that need for sentimentality?

As every social historian knows, great populations of children and bonded servants were treated no better than the majority of slaves. And a slave auction, like the epidemic of indiscriminate violence, disease, and cussedness—not to mention massive drunkenness, in which soldiers were scooped up "promiscuously" on the day after—was too common to be taken as seriously as most of us today would have liked . . . or as the most rabid Abolitionists would have liked, for they were geographically almost as distant from that particular evil as we are temporally.

Such knowledge is the penalty anthropologists and social historians pay for their prurient interest in the Past. No matter how fascinated we are by those alien cultures, we will eventually come upon unassailable evidence of their limitations, their inhumanity, their stupidity, their utter insensitivity and (by present-day standards) viciousness. No one escapes, with the possible exceptions of those vague and distant penumbral cultures, about which so little is known that they couldn't possibly be indicted for any criminal attitude or act. But of course, it is our ignorance that lends the mists of enchantment to them, for if we knew them better, we can be sure that they'd prove to be as glaringly, humanly flawed as ourselves. When Stephen Daedalus is being quizzed by a school administrator in *Ulysses*, he tells that smug and self-satisfied functionary something that is possessed of a horrible yet fascinating truth; he says, "History is a nightmare from which I'm trying to awake."

Were people aware of their own brutality at this time? It is fashionable, as well as tempting, to say that they were not; but the fact is, there is a whiff of casual malice in the way that injuries and deaths were reported, especially if the victims were poor. Consider poor Mrs. Murphy, who, by mistake, drank rat poison, and "in fifteen minutes she was a corpse." There is something a bit jaunty about that report, as it is stated; it might have even verged upon being funny, since the woman had an Irish name, and Irish corpses were much funnier than most other kinds.

❦   Now I have brought you back, and have introduced you to the turmoil and confusion that you were promised at the beginning. It would be possible to go on to page four, where there are three columns of reports that are admirably rich in chaos, rapine, and slaughter. But if I were to quote from these, I would have to balance them out with ads for cod liver oil, business cards, snuff, eyeglasses, photographs, carpets, train tickets to Pittsburgh and Philadelphia, and even elastic roofing (whatever that might have been).

I would also have to mention Constitution Water, which promises a cure for dyspepsia, suppressed menstration, and diabetes. In proof of the last, the testimonial of J.V.L. DeWitt, of Danville, Pa., is cited. In it, he swears that for five months before his cure, he passed over two gallons of water every 24 hours.

Well, it is good to know that DeWitt recovered, and it's a shame that modern medicine has lost the secret embodied in Constitution Water. From all the evidence in these newspapers, it must have been a simpler world back then; and maybe diseases were simpler, as well. But this can't be quite true, because it's hard to draw a line around the editorial policy of the Journal. I guess what we'll have to conclude is that, this was in truth a simpler world back then; but this simplicity wasn't just any sort of simplicity, it was one that was murky, self-contradictory, and confused.

The more we think about it, the more familiar it all begins to seem. After reading these papers for a while, you want to go back to a good, neat, reasonably argued textbook, so that you can find out what all of this turmoil and confusion were really about. All complicated territories need simple maps; and—as this essay which I have just written is intended to demonstrate—vice versa.

*Getting America
Down on Paper*

Several years ago I advertised for a signed, first-edition copy of Thomas Hart Benton's *An Artist in America* (New York, 1937), and soon received a quotation for a copy priced at $30.00. It was listed in good condition, but without dust jacket.

Prices quoted in response to a "wanted-to-buy" ad are often higher than general retail prices, because by advertising you betray an active desire to purchase, which alters the character of the transaction; but even so, this quote seemed a bit steep, so I decided to wait, hoping to receive a lower one. When another week passed without an offer, however, I ordered the book, received it as advertised, and was content. The transaction, I assumed, was over.

But shortly afterwards, I received another quote, offering a signed copy for just $12.50, in the original dust jacket. After some ritualistic cussing, I ordered it, received it promptly, and found that—unlike the first copy I'd bought—this was the "Special Missouri Edition," with Benton's name written on a tipped-in leaf announcing the fact.

As for the rest of the book, it was identical to the regular trade edition, so far as I could see—it was published by Robert M. McBride & Co., bound in blue cloth, with 276 pages of text, and liberally illustrated with over sixty of Benton's inimitable, wild, cranky, cartoon-style drawings. I concluded that some enterprising Missouri slicker had bought up a few hundred trade copies, talked Benton into signing leaves with the "Special Missouri Edition" business printed on it (along with a short notice that Benton was from Missouri, in case you missed the point), then tipped these leaves into the trade edition, right before the title pages. (Such "tipped in" pages are glued to the inner edge so that they look like part of the original book.)

I admire a person who's enterprising, and don't in the least begrudge this anonymous operator his or her moment of cunning, along with the profits reaped therefrom. It's not a bad idea; and ideas that are not-bad should be put to work. I especially didn't object in this case, for I was able to purchase the fruits of the enterprise for only $12.50. Of course, if I'd been possessed of more foresight and/or character, I would not have spent that thirty dollars for the other copy; but I have long ago forgiven myself, realizing that I might just as easily have lost thirty dollars on some race horse named Tumbleweed or Prickly Heat.

I find little in the story of this transaction for pride. No doubt one should buy rare books with a certain aloof and calculating reserve; but when it comes to books, I am deficient in such qualities, for I am motivated more by passion than commercial prudence. Still, I hereby offer my original copy, without dust jacket, for $30.00. It's not a stupendous bargain, but it's a whole lot better than six $5 tickets on Tumbleweed or Prickly Heat to win, as I hope to demonstrate in what follows.

But first, you will have noticed that I have slyly avoided reference to the mystery at the heart of this account. I have avoided any reference to purpose. I have skirted the question of why anyone might want to buy a signed copy of Benton's autobiography at any price. It is not really a famous book; therefore, why should one seek out a signed first edition? Why should anyone even want to read it?

For me, the answer to these questions is quite simple: Benton's *An Artist in America* provided one of the wonderful experiences of my youth. I have never, throughout all the ensuing decades, ceased thinking about it for long; and it was to memorialize and symbolize this fact that I made an effort several years ago to buy a signed copy.

I first read it when I was a student at North High School, in Columbus, and was so enthusiastic that I recommended it to my good pal, Bill Evans, who was a genuine artistic prodigy. (Evans still lives in central Ohio, and is still painting—possibly at this very moment.) Bill read it and responded very much as I did; in fact, for years afterwards he quoted from Benton's account of his initiation into sex, which reads as follows: "One night my virginity was taken by a black-haired young slut who wore a flaming red kimono and did her hair in curls like a little girl." When we read this passage we were approximately the same age as Benton was when the great event itself took place. In the solid, middle class, midwestern neighborhoods of that time, this passed for pretty gamy stuff; and the adult world that loomed over us seemed puritanical and restrictive beyond the wildest imagining of today's youth.

But what about the adults in Benton's day? Judging from his testimony, and assuming that he was in any way representative, they might as well have thrown in the towel, because here is an autobiography of a man who never outgrew his adolescence—if growing up entails a loss of vitality and exuberance. The book is filled with wonderful stories about Benton's people back in rural Missouri before the turn of the century, about himself and his artist friends, and about what he saw and learned from his picaresque adventures while, first, trying out the Bohemian life in Chicago, New York, and Paris, and then bumming around the United States with a sketch pad, when he really did, in his own way, discover the America of his time.

As a boy I liked to draw and had occasional seizures of ambition to be a painter, an "artist." I had seen reproductions of Benton's paintings; and learning of his book, I was curious and got a copy from the library to read. It did not help me become a painter, for I had no real talent; but ironically, it did give me a sense of how life can be lived adventurously if you learn how to look at the things about you; and its celebration of life in all of its wonderful capaciousness and energetic vulgarity was an important factor in my wanting to become a novelist, a poet, an essayist, "a writer."

Although I did not then know the word, what I was experiencing was in its way a typically proletarian work—and yet, Benton's proletarianism was stamped with his own personality; and it was further distinguished by being of the home-grown sort—wholesome, ungrudging, honest, and sentimental—devoid of those earnest and arid abstractions of so much imported socialist theory, but as real and familiar as the odor of stogies at old-time midwestern Fourth of July bean dinners, where they had flags draped over the lecture platform railings, beauty queens, hog calling contests, county chairmen, state representatives, gravelly voiced old farmers and their prim wives, along with plenty of bisquits, mashed potatoes, peas, fried chicken . . . and big dishes of soup beans with pork, cooked in honor of the Civil War veterans, who had lived on such cheap though sturdy fare back in the days when they were soldier boys.

The opening pages of *An Artist in America* are simply wonderful; they are charged with what, in another context, Benton refers to as "the *go* that electrifies existence." From the first words, we are aware of the vitality of the man whose testimony is before us—there is no lid that could keep all of him in. He wrote as he painted, with unmatched vigor and reckless comic shrewdness that cast all that he saw in a new light. Nevertheless, the American heartland that he knew and celebrated is recognizable, for it is related to that of Mark Twain, Sherwood Anderson, Irvin S. Cobb, Jesse Stuart, and dozens of other common, local types who have loved the rural traditions in all their native toughness, bizarre convolutions of manner, and cantankerous common sense.

And yet, although Benton's embrace of what is called "folk culture" in his famous paintings and murals is how he is best remembered, his family was far from being brutishly ignorant. Along with their earthy realism, they possessed something dangerously close to genteel dignity. And while Benton makes it clear that in that time and place culture was measured by the standards of "women who were offended by tobacco spit in the fireplace," there was more to it than this, for his father even tried to get him to study Latin.

But the lad proved unfit—not through lack of brains, but through simple down-home stubborn wrong-headedness. And the reader can't help wondering if the old man had resorted to reverse psychology and nagged the young cuss to become a painter, he might well have turned out to be an accomplished Latin scholar.

This was a curious world, and Benton himself has trouble getting it exactly right. "With the first families in the west," he wrote, "gentility was not so much a matter of actual conduct as of attitude." There is much truth in this statement, of course; but it is a truth that is hardly limited to the folks Benton knew in Missouri all those years ago.

His father was a lawyer and politician, good enough to be sent to Washington, a place which young Tom didn't much like or take to. Understandably, his father wanted his boy to be a lawyer like himself, and keep up the family tradition (the other famous Thomas Hart Benton, a U.S. Senator, was his great uncle); but here, as with Latin, Tom balked. He was too wild, too headstrong, too full of "an exuberant youthful pugnacity."

This last was no doubt somewhat compensatory. As if to correct any wrong impression people might have concerning his artistic pretensions, he was always a tough little bantam brawler. Later, during World War I, he became a prize fighter in the navy and after that had a small part as a pug in an early silent film. But from a parental viewpoint, he had been given too many "opportunities for gaudy self-expression," and there was no taming him. Actually, he wasn't entirely unqualified for the law, and states the problem clearly, saying that he "was argumentative enough but . . . could not be induced to study and . . . had a low taste for creekbank company."

The low company his dad could forgive, but when his boy decided he wanted to become an artist, the old man was distressed, for he associated artists with pimps. As for his great moment of decision: Benton says he was standing in a tavern one night, gazing at the painting of a nude behind the bar, and some other young fellows started jeering at him. Although he was still in his teens, Benton was not ruffled; on the spur of the moment he announced that he himself was an artist, by God, and he was not gazing up at that painting of that nude woman with the lust of a common bumpkin, but with professional interest.

Having announced the fact, there was nothing else to do but go ahead and corroborate it . . . which is to say go ahead and become an artist, which he did. Of course the yearning had already been there, just waiting for some louts in a saloon to challenge his over-attentiveness to the painting of a naked woman. And that yearning was richly justified: his gift for being excited by appearances, along with the common folk all around him, fills his book with light. Benton drew and painted pictures in order to learn what the world looked like.

His gift was authentic, but he still showed a flair for aesthetic posturing. "Having determined to become an artist," he wrote, "I bought a black shirt, a red tie, and a pair of peg-top corduroy pants. I wore this outfit with a derby hat which, when I let my hair grow, sat high on my head. I began to be regarded as a genius among my companions—my garb was proof of it."

Such posturing was not only fun, it was dangerous. It led Benton to Chicago, then New York, where he associated with the Stieglitz group for a while (with their "aesthetic pose and lunatic conviction"), and where he led so interesting and Bohemian a life that he even managed to get stabbed by a girlfriend.

Eventually, he settled down and proposed to an Italian-American girl, whose father could not speak English. When he learned that Benton wanted to marry his daughter, the old man came to visit him in his studio, and—since he couldn't speak English and Benton couldn't speak Italian— sat there all day watching his future son-in-law paint. When evening came, the old man stood up, politely shook Benton's hand, and departed. Soon after, the marriage took place, and one can't help observing that, truly, there are far less sensible and civilized rituals for acquiring in-laws.

Neither marriage, nor World War I, nor the Great Depression slowed Benton down. He traveled everywhere, without evident means of support, meeting all sorts of people, soaking in the secret geographies of the land, looking at everything with passionate attentiveness and drawing it. His discovery of the miraculous shapes of the industrial machinery that re- pelled others was a personal revelation and marked a great turn in his career, for it signified the shift of his aesthetics from the conventionalized romantic artist's reliance upon "inspiration," or things within, to the powerful reality, stubborn honesty, and dumb glory of the world without. Everything was there for the seeing, and Benton looked and drew until his head and sketchpads were full.

Nothing he saw was beneath his interest, and the titles of the illustrations convey the fact: "Red River Landing" (complete with steamboat), "The Open Hearth" (workers in a steel mill), "The Woman Preacher," "Swing- ing Bridge," "Father and Daughter" (he with a fiddle, she with a guitar), "Burlesque Girl," "Bughouse," "Cotton Pickers," "Oyster House Music," "Honky tonk," and "Oil Town." His illustrations and stories add up to a rich proletarian feast; but they are really more than that: they are in their very own way an artistic triumph—shrewd, humorous, and utterly unique.

In these pages you will find just about as much life as could ever be packed into a single book, conveying a sense of gusty enjoyment and a cussed and riotous innocence. And what a triumph it is, when one consid- ers all of that America Benton had set out to find, what he saw of it and how much of it he understood . . . how much he "got down on paper," as the saying goes—a saying that is here meant in both ways, for Benton wrote pretty much as he drew. He got it all down on paper in both ways, with a style all his own, and every line of it was spectacularly worth doing.

🍎 *Old Laughs*

I remember years ago, coming upon an observation by William Dean Howells to the effect that when he was a young man, he had concluded that two people should not marry unless they came from the same country; later, he decided that it would be better if they came from the same state; but finally, in his old age, he had come to the conclusion that it would be best if they came from the same township.

This seems to me a partial truth, at best, but a very deep one. It is disturbing in its implicit acknowledgement of the authority of particularity in the form of region and locale—who wants to contemplate such exiguous limitations? But independent of what we *want*, there is the unquestionable fact that people from radically different backgrounds have demonstrated, not the limitations of background, but of Howell's formula. To put the matter negatively: I would be willing to bet that the incidence of divorce among couples who've come from the same township is pretty much the same as that of other marriages.

So much, you might think, for William Dean Howells. And why would anyone bother to quote him, anyway, when nine out of ten people couldn't identify him or name one novel he wrote; and those who do know something about him, probably think of him primarily as a friend of Mark Twain, whoever he was. But reputations are communal judgments, and judgments are not truths, they are . . . well, *judgments*. Furthermore, and for the record, Howells did write at least one great novel, *A Modern Instance;* and for this alone should be better known among the American reading public. All twenty-six of them.

The partial truthfulness of Howells' uncharacteristically cynical observation is evident, but I also claimed depth for it. How can something be partial and deep? Well, it's easy. While the exceptions to the prescription for an intimately shared background as a prerequisite for a good marriage are many, the idea is nevertheless possessed of a kind of legitimacy.

Some kind of shared background is essential for sustained intimacy, and sustained intimacy is what a marriage is essentially supposed to be.

But in judging Howells' judgment, we have to think of how language is always a function of time, and we have to understand how the world has altered since Howells said this—whenever he did say it, if in fact he did say it at all. Life in the United States has of course changed enormously since he was alive to give voice to such an idea. The terms "marriage" and "township" have changed significantly; and of course, whatever might be meant by the words "successful marriage" must in some ways be far different today from what it was then. Sustained intimacy, we might say, is no longer confined to people who have grown up practically within shouting distance of each other. For one thing, such old-fashioned neighborhoods scarcely exist any longer. No matter how it may have degenerated in other ways, the world is no longer as insular as it once was; it has expanded beyond the wildest dreams of yesterday's wise men—a truism which every commencement speaker will remind us of this spring.

But Howells' argument is also interesting in ways that have nothing specific to do with marriage—which is fortunate in the present circumstance, since my subject is not marriage at all, but humor.

To approach humor through a reference to Twain's good friend William Dean Howells—not to mention the subject of marriage—is something of a bold stroke, if I do say so myself. What do marriage and humor have in common? Well, a shared intimacy, of course. Both are forms of shared intimacy, and like some wines and many children, they often do not travel well.

The effectiveness of a joke is so intricately part of the language and environment, so subtly a matter of connotation, voice, tone, timing, and nuance, that it's a wonder a joke can survive even that minimal transition from teller to auditor. In fact, sometimes it doesn't. To refer to Twain once again—for he had opinions on everything, which includes humor: he once stated that the effectiveness of a joke depended upon five one-millionths of a second timing . . . which was funnier when he said it than it is now, because during his lifetime there was no technology for measuring so nicely. No, the more I think of it, the more impossible the whole matter seems, so that I'm almost tempted to conclude that, theoretically, jokes simply can't exist. It's almost enough to make you laugh.

But, they do exist, and we all know it. We enjoy them. We hear them all the time, and tell them to others. They lighten the moment for us, and there's hardly a moment around anywhere which doesn't need lightening. I use the word "lighten," of course, in both its signification to "make less ponderous and grave," as well as to brighten the place where one stands, so that objects can be seen better. I use it in both its levitating and visual sense.

As for the first, it seems to me significant that we can speak of a body's center of gravity, but not of some "center of levity." Why not? Apparently levity cannot be thought of as having a center. Levity is, after all, a relative weightlessness—and how can weightlessness be said to have a focus of highest density as if it were a mass? It is as if jokes were all spirit, all air. And yet, every joke must have a point. Then, isn't a joke's point its center? Well, sure, maybe . . . sort of.

Well, let's leave it there, wherever it is, and go on to more interesting, though scarcely less puzzling, matters. When I speak of the bewildering limitations of such factors as voice, tone, intonation, value systems, timing, and nuance, I am acknowledging the provincial, even parochial, character of humor. Like some wines, those other spirits referred to—not to mention children, those spirited homunculi that surround us in every direction except time and get even with us for having once been children ourselves— jokes often really do not travel well.

There is even a class of jokes about this fact. Such jokes have to do with the Englishman's proverbial slow-wittedness in picking up on things. The most brilliant of these is a set of limericks (the point of the whole business being the second limerick, which is the Englishman's botched version of the first), the first of which begins: "There once was a fellow named Skinner." Unfortunately, this is too gross for repetition here, so I'll go on with my argument.

The stereotype of the Englishman's bulky, trundling, arthritic humor isn't really deserved, of course, for all it means is simply that Englishmen don't always share *our* sort of humor. And whatever the validity of this principle at one time, it is certainly less true today than it may have been in the past, largely because of the relentless, compulsive, multi-national sharing generated by television, and film.

But insofar as it remains true, how disheartening it is to think that two

nations that speak more-or-less the same language have a humor barrier—
a sort of irony curtain, you might say. We can support each other in
adventures undertaken in the name of the protection of our national rights
in the Falkland Islands or in Libya, but we can't seem to get the same
joke in the same way.

❦   Several paragraphs back I stated that my subject was not
marriage, but humor; and now I will state that it is not about national and
linguistic differences in humor, as the immediate foregoing might suggest,
but about humor in time. And I promise no more tricks: this really is my
subject, and I will not deceive you again.

These matters are, of course, not totally unconnected. Language, like
all things, exists in space and time, and jokes are part of language. They are
sub-sets in the class of language games—individual games that conform to
their own sets of rules. If they do not conform to such rules, we wouldn't
recognize them as jokes at all, but think of them as anecdotes or comments
or observations. One sub-set of the sub-set of jokes is the shaggy dog
story, which—like certain deconstructionist views of literature—exists
against the set of conventions it is ostensibly a part of, and paradoxically
plays the game by seeming to play it at first, but ending up not actually
doing so at all. The joke, it turns out, is upon the listener as well as upon
the conventions of the game.

It is of course important to distinguish jokes from humor, which is a
larger and less-defined entity. Perhaps it is because it is less defined that
it lasts longer—as if it were not so locked into a specific form, and never
having been the fashion of a day, as jokes usually are, it is enabled to last
on for years.

Mark Twain would be the inevitable example of a humorist whose
utterances often seem as fresh today as when they were first uttered . . . or
written. But though he was exceptional, Twain was not really an exception.
That is to say, he was not alone in his time; he was only one of many gifted
humorists who wrote and lectured and kept them rolling in the aisles for
several decades after the Civil War. One of these others was Petroleum
V. Nasby (David Ross Locke), who was said to have done much to lighten

the dark days of Lincoln's presidency. Unfortunately, Nasby lived much of his life in Ohio.

Another famous humorist of the time was Bill Nye. There is a passage in *Bill Nye's Chestnuts* (Chicago, 1888) which is strikingly like Mark Twain's finest efforts, and deserves quoting. The piece from which the following is quoted is titled, "The Romance of Horse-Shoeing":

> The bronco is full of spirit, and, although docile under ordinary circumstances, he will at times get enthusiastic, and do things which he afterward, in his sober moments, bitterly regrets.
>
> Some broncos have formed the habit of bucking. They do not all buck. Only those that are alive do so. When they are dead they are more subdued and gentle.
>
> A bronco often becomes so attached to his master that he will lay down his life if necessary. His master's life, I mean.

❧   This strikes me as very good and worthy of Twain at his best. *Near* best, anyway. But since Nye wasn't born until 1850, he wasn't ripe enough for the Civil War or for amusing Lincoln when he needed it . . . and beyond doubt, he learned a great deal from his elders—people like Mark Twain, Petroleum V. Nasby, and a dozen others.

But I still haven't been able to settle down; I haven't been able to get to my true subject. Some insidious force is at work keeping me from it, centrifugal forces operating against the levity of my destination. *As* for this subject, it is that particular form of humor that is embodied in generic, which is to say, traditional jokes, or "jests" as they were once called.

Specifically, I have a story to tell about twenty or thirty books—most of them classifiable as jest books—that I bought years ago out in the country near Albany, Ohio. These books were old, their dates extending from the sixteenth century (e.g., *Comicorum Graecorum Sententiae*, printed somewhere in Bavaria in 1569 by a man named "Henricus Stephanus"—from the evidence, nobody ever knew anything about him) to a handful of early nineteenth-century facetiae—several of these being variant editions of the same book, *Joe Miller's Jests: Or, the Wit's Vade Mecum.* The latest of these was published in London in 1838. If they had been in decent condition, this box of books would have been quite valuable; as it was, however, they had been sadly neglected, and many of their pages were blackened with mold smear and their bindings bloated and discolored from the dark, dank atmosphere of an old barn or shed.

The 1838 copy of *Joe Miller's Jests*, however, is an exception. It is in good condition, all 153 pages of it; and, like most jest books, it is small—scarcely larger than a pack of cards. (In the world of early printings, it is as if only such serious subjects as theology, philosophy, geography, and perhaps travel, were considered worthy of the large quartos and folios.) 1838 also represents a very late reprint, for there once was a real Joe Miller—a comic actor who had died exactly one hundred years before, in 1738, and the first jest book that bore his name came out a year later.

This book was so popular that it was reprinted many times, newer editions often featuring new jests, so that the number of jokes in my 1838 edition is significantly greater than the original 247. But most of the original jokes remained throughout all those printings, and there was once a time that whenever a sad old gag of any sort was trotted out, it was referred to as "a Joe Miller." But by now, that sad old reference to sad old gags has itself evaporated, no longer possessed of even the dignity of a cliché.

Although he had virtually nothing to do with the book, Joe Miller must have been an interesting character. Apparently, he was illiterate; thus, one is forced to make two assumptions: he didn't write down any of these jokes so that after his death they could be collected in a book bearing his name, and he learned his lines as a comic actor either by ear or by guess. As for this latter conclusion, maybe both. Probably, it didn't make too much difference so far as Joe's audience was concerned, providing he didn't mess up a punch line.

Not having the first edition of the *Vade Mecum,* I can't judge the relative merits of the jests according to their age. It's hard to know whether the worst jokes are those that have been added, those that have stubbornly remained, or perhaps a mixture of old and new. Please note that I did not refer to "the best" jests, and there is a reason for this—there aren't any. The book is a compendium of just about the most miserable excuses for jokes that one can imagine; and some exceed all imagination in their utter, uncompromising, down-home wretchedness.

Consider the following: a dying woman asks her husband to help her make a will, but he declines, saying, "No, Madam, you have had your will all your lifetime, and now I will have mine." (Obviously, these two were from different townships.) A man being said to have died insolvent evokes the reply: "Died insolvent! That's a lie, for he died in England, I am sure, for I was at his burying." Then there's the one about a sergeant who was attacked by a dog, whereupon he killed him with his sword. When the dog's owner asked him why he hadn't struck the beast with "the blunt end of his halbert," the sergeant replied that he would indeed have used the blunt end of his halbert if the dog had attacked him with its tail.

These lamentable jests have not been sought out with shameful ardor and plucked from the text simply in order to sully Joe Miller's name and denigrate an almost totally forgotten reputation—the three referred to above are taken from facing pages; and it is sad to report that their dismal and pathetic inadequacy is near to being representative. They are representative in both quality and type; two of them (as do most of those remaining) depend for their humor upon puns that strike the modern reader as verging upon dim-wittedness . . . not simply the dim-wittedness of the characters who are word-befuddled, but of any conceivable reader who might find them funny. (Having stated this, however, I do have to admit that the one about the Soldier and the Dog strikes me as pretty good.)

Not that puns can't be delicious—of course they can, for they depend upon a playfulness that most of the world sadly needs. They also reveal a second view—usually irrelevant in the narrow sense—that affords an immediately ironic perspective into the material reference of an utterance. Furthermore, puns often have an eerie or oblique relevance because of a concealed linguistic affinity, in that the words confused share a common root. This can be true of sophisticated puns as well as their opposite. It is the case with the first jest quoted above, where the unbereaved husband plays upon the word "will" in its reference to a legal instrument directing the dispersal of property after one's death along with its more common, broader signification as a determination that something should come about or be so. The words are, of course, the same in origin, and their shared identity is so transparent that the wordplay in Joe Miller's old book would prove embarrassing if one were to try it out in polite company today.

For all his quondam notoriety, Joe Miller is today a somewhat ghostly figure, more symbol than substance. Bits of information crop up in obvious places, but they are largely duplicative and exiguous . . . which is to say, largely small. Evidently, little is known about him. The most interesting account I've read is a short essay by Robertson Davies, the Canadian novelist and man of letters, in his book of prose pieces, *A Voice From the Attic* (Knopf, 1960). Most of the generally available information is to be found in Mr. Davies' essay, along with a few quoted jests from the original and—as would be expected from this writer—lively and perceptive commentary. He ends his piece with cautionary advice, as follows: "Let us beware of a superior weariness in examining these few jokes from the original 247; it is their form rather than their substance which makes them different from the kind of thing we read and hear every day."

My admiration for Robertson Davies' opinions is very great; I have gained pleasure and wisdom from reading his fiction and essays. I consider him a writer of rare depth and intellectual range, so it is a pleasure to disagree with him. He reminds us that Joe Miller's jokes are not the gold of his age, but the copper pennies. So much is evident; but this does not alter the fact that these jests are ineffably dreary. Scholarship, tolerance, and historical perspective can do only so much—these jokes are wretched.

But what is the reason for such a wealth of impoverishment? Why are they so bad? How could a book, gathering increments as solemn and heavy-witted as the originals through the years, sustain such great popularity for so long, striking people from generation to generation as a cause for mirth? (It should be admitted that "Joe Miller's" were the source of much groaning, as I have stated above; but still, these books were reprinted for a century and a half, which fact implies at least a chronic estimate of popularity, in an age without public opinion polls other than the actual sales of books.) *Were* people in those dark times actually more fog-brained and stupid than the great public of today? A brief contemplation of the average television sit-com makes this hard to believe. And perhaps there is a faint whiff of an answer in this commonly noted fact that whatever is banal and silly in pop culture has found its rightful place in the ever popular scapegoat of television. What would we have to kick around if it were done away with? The answer to this hypothetical question might turn out to be: a new edition of Joe Miller's jest book.

But jest books are a thing of the past; they seem incompatible with high-tech-cult. They simply aren't published today. What use would they have? If you want gags, watch late-night television (the latest comedy hour featuring the latest young and up-coming comics). Jest books no longer have a role to play in a whizz-bang, media-muddled, electronically gagged world. They don't belong in the late twentieth century any more than they could be conceived of as belonging (at least in our ethnocentric view) to other cultures. Irony curtain notwithstanding, there is something intrinsically English or American about them, just as they seem to fit naturally in the period between the first Queen Elizabeth and the world of Teddy Roosevelt. Who could imagine a jest book in modern Japanese? Or Swedish? A command performance of a "Bob Hope Special" in Stockholm was recently televised, and it was in every way as bad as Joe Miller's Jest Book. Not even the appearance of Liv Ullman helped liven it up; but, if I remember correctly, she didn't tell any jokes. No, there is something intrinsic to English/American culture in Joe Miller's pathetic little book, and—to misquote the popular song about New York, as it wallows in its own disgusting brand of parochial self-congratulation verging upon social narcissism—if it can't make it here, it can't make it anywhere.

The favorite butts of many of Joe Miller's jokes through the years are Irishmen and Welshmen. The Irish have had greater lasting power than the Welsh when it comes to being on the wrong end of comedy; the Welsh aren't all that visible, and today the average American would hardly know what to satirize, or accept as funny, in a Welshman. When you get past Richard Burton and Dylan Thomas, who have you got? And what do *they* have in common that people could satirize, except hard drinking and generally tough behavior, which are of course territories already staked out by their fellow Celts just across the Irish Sea?

But the comic Irishman with his irrepressible bounce can still be recognized, as in the little story that Joe (or one of his anonymous editors) tells, concerning the young love-stricken Pat or Mike who was so tormented by longing for a lady of great riches that, as he said, "he couldn't sleep for dreaming of her."

Relatively, this isn't too bad. For Joe Miller, it's A-minus, or perhaps even A. And, although it's still not the sort of thing to lighten a dismal winter's day, it is a considerable improvement over the story about a

Welshman, who had worked as a carpenter in Bristol, where he managed to save 12 shillings. (To understand this joke, we have to understand three things: the Welsh were supposed to pronounce "b" as "p"; they were supposed to say "hur" for almost any pronoun, including "our," "it," and "I"—try to figure this out; I can't—and they were an object of mirth because they were poor.) "Ah, poor Pristow," said the Welshman as he left town, "if one or more of hur countrymen were to give hur such another shake as hur has done, it would be poor Pristow, indeed."

❦   The best things in Joe's jest book are not, properly speaking, jests at all, but the little rhymes at the end. Some of these are actually, or almost actually, funny. Consider this epitaph on a wife:

> Beneath lies my wife
> Whose death is my life.

Not brilliant, but not bad. (Obviously, wives joined Irishmen and Welshmen as objects of ridicule and scorn—although their misery is not compounded, so far as I know, since I can't remember a single barb aimed at an Irish or Welsh wife.)

An epitaph on a miser is much sharper:

> Reader, beware immoderate love of pelf;
> Here lies the worst of thieves—who robb'd himself.

That for a prizefighter sounds a note that is wistful, and with a hint of the tragic:

> His thrust like lightning flew, yet subtle death
> Parried them all, and beat him out of breath.

But my favorite is titled "To a Bad Fiddler":

> Old Orpheus played so well he moved old Nick,
> Whilst thou mov'st nothing but thy fiddle-stick.

Many of these pieces—rhymes and jests both—go back to the time of Swift; but the quaint old expression "Fiddlesticks!"—meaning nonsense or folly—was familiar at least a century before the bad fiddler was lampooned, and this fact unquestionably added to the pleasure that a contemporary might have gotten from the couplet.

The rhymes live, while the jests lie amould'ring on the page (in many of my copies, both literally and figuratively). Why should the rhymes survive while the jests die? Partly, no doubt, through the intrinsic grace of rhyming, with rhymes which are old enough to strike us as quaint, and even melodious in their way; while the puns, being self-consciously clever and yet obvious, have lost all claim to wit or charm.

Language is constantly changing and expanding, so it is not likely that we will ever run out of good puns, which is to say fresh confusions of terms. New facts, new people, new words, new technologies—all are part of the growing language, and as they expand, so do opportunities for punning grow with them. I need only refer to that shameless groaner referring to radical differences between British and American humor— "an irony curtain." Pretty awful, certainly; and not the sort of thing to pin a statesman's fame upon . . . and yet, before Winston Churchill made his famous "Iron Curtain" speech in 1946 the pun would have been meaningless—which is to say, not a pun at all.

But for all its changes and all its expansive energy, the English language has remained fairly stable throughout the centuries. No sentence can possibly mean the same thing twice; but given this important philosophical and linguistic truth, one must also add that the words Shakespeare used— though spoken quite differently in his time and never quite meaning what they mean today—have remained sufficiently stable that the plays can still be performed with spectacular results, even ignoring Elizabethan pronunciation . . . which if spoken faithfully, would, in fact, render much of the speech incomprehensible to the average modern audience.

If one might conceive of a language as a system that is stable and unchanging, created in an instant, then there is a time limit for the playing out of all the puns available in it. This is a sort of entropy—the yet-unfound puns representing potential energy that is expended, or translated into kinetic energy, the instant that pun is "made," with subsequent loss of total available energy in the system. Repetitions of these puns will evoke diminishing pleasurable surprise and discovery, so that the audible or rhetorical groans that often accompany a decent pun will eventually merge into the silent groans that await those that have become trite and dull.

In short, there is a class of puns intrinsic to the language that have been played out, exhausted, used-up. Hard as it is to believe, some of Joe Miller's most awful and leaden puns must have had a first, fresh, electric connection that jolted an audience into real laughter. But a humor that relies upon such innovations is possessed of a dwindling capital, and the traces of its expenditure (you will note that I have launched upon an utterly impossible metaphor) can be found upon the leaves of a hundred or more editions of old Joe Miller's Jest Books, most of which go by other names. Which somehow seems only appropriate under the circumstances.

The puns that Joe and his many imitators have found so durable as a form of humor are not intrinsically frivolous. There was a time, in the ancient world, when language was supposed to bear some intrinsic relationship to reality. This premise is not totally devoid of ingenuity, for the early Wittgenstein (he who wrote *Tractatus Logico Philosophicus*) language provided pictures of reality that had to be accurate or they could not lead to effective behavior. Unquestionably, this is true: but there are not only different languages, there are different *sorts* of languages; and all of them provide pictures of reality that have some claim to accuracy, although each does it in its own way.

Unfortunately, the truths of comparative linguistics were not available to the ancients, no matter how wise they were; and they were therefore beguiled into thinking that there was a more intimate relationship between words and things than most of us believe today. Given such a situation, the coincidence of one word suddenly jumping into the place of another that sounded like it was always to some extent a revelation. Puns were not exclusively the occasion for humor, but sometimes of awe: it was as if the gods had spoken out of the secret language that underlies the one we think we know. Such occasions were dignified by a word that has none of the frolicsome brevity of the word "pun"; they were instances of paronomasia, which is not the same sort of thing at all, for it has five syllables against one.

Perhaps the day is near when that which had at one time degenerated into mere punning will be restored to its original (whether real or fancied) dignity. Perhaps from the very beginning, through the treble silliness of its operations there has been a diapason of somber bass notes, dense with gravity, whether centered or diffused, awaiting only its discovery. Perhaps underlying Joe Miller's jests, there is a mysterious ontological code, which awaits only the key for its fullest revelation.

Certainly, there is more than levity at work in all this. Could it really have been a need for laughter that drove so many people from so many different generations to the pages of this Vade Mecum? Is it possible that daily life was so miserable for the majority that they could find relief in such jests as these?

This is a gruesome thought, best not dwelt upon. But there is one virtue that shines like a jewel in this setting, though it would be no more than a lump of coal in most. While many books promise well and end badly, Joe Miller's old jest book doesn't promise anything but the freedom and release from the sober march of jests that beckons to the reader from the book's termination. And yet, that ending itself is rather stylish in its own way—appropriate for dull jest books, and tedious perorations alike, so I will use it myself, here and now. It is an epitaph in Stepney Church-yard that goes as follows:

> Here lies the body of John Saul,
> Spital-fields weaver, and that's all.

 *The Green Hills of Hemingway*

When I was a young writer in the early 1950's I shared in the prevailing admiration for the stories of Ernest Hemingway. I took pleasure in his work, and took additional pleasure in the pleasure which his work brought to so many people. Since writers tend to be instinctive loners, spending long hours in silent travail with language and ideas, it is perhaps only natural that they can occasionally find a special satisfaction in having some share in large and public enthusiams.

Hemingway was still very much alive in those days; and he was at that time more famous than at any other period of his life—although most of his memorable work was behind him. The only major book he had not yet written by 1952 was *The Old Man and the Sea*, which *Life Magazine* then brought out in a single full-length issue, breaking long precedent in doing so, and celebrating the fame of a man who had become as famous as the movie stars he liked to associate with.

If, as a writer, Hemingway was an instinctive loner, he certainly managed to conceal the fact, and did so with panache. But, of course, the celebrity was simply the public man; whereas, Hemingway the writer worked in silence, alone inside his language, just as all of us have to do it. And yet, with Hemingway, the idea of loneliness seems irrelevant, for there have been few writers so lionized as he was in his last years; he had become almost the celebrity Mark Twain had been half a century before. And Twain did not have movie stars and other mad media creations to compete with. Certainly, no writer has been so celebrated since Hemingway's death. Today, most of the great celebrities are television personalities, sports figures, rock stars, and other non-cerebral (or, at least, non-literary) types.

But back then it was different. It was almost as if Hemingway had been invented for *Life Magazine*. . . or *vice versa*. So I naturally read *The Old*

Man and the Sea when it came out, and found it almost as good as it was supposed to be. What pleasure and what relief this was! Wasn't it good that Hemingway "still had it," as he himself might have said . . . and probably *did* say, for he had learned to imitate Ernest Hemingway, the celebrity, better than anyone else.

But nothing is forever; and not quite ten years later, there was that ugly, dismal, wintry scene in Idaho. The initial story was that "Pappa" had killed himself while cleaning his shotgun. It is doubtful if many people ever really believed this; and, eventually, of course, it was understood by everyone that Ernest Hemingway—a sick old man before his time—had committed suicide, just as his own pappa had done so many years before.

🐝　　　I had already begun to collect Hemingway's first editions when, in 1964, my own first book of short stories, *Bitter Knowledge*, was published by Scribner's, which was Hemingway's publisher. As a Scribner's author, I was sent one of the first copies of *A Moveable Feast*, which I naturally began to read with great interest.

But from the beginning I realized that things were not the same. Here, in his first posthumous book, Hemingway gave voice to opinions that were often shockingly insensitive, and, at times, simply grubby. In his petty and malicious comments about his old pal F. Scott Fitzgerald, for example, Hemingway proved to have been no more than the coldest and most sinister of acquaintances. Here was obviously a very complex, and obviously very imperfect, human being—a decade's colorful testimony by *Life Magazine* notwithstanding.

Still, it is somewhat surprising that I was surprised. Shouldn't I have known better? Yeats claimed that one must choose between perfection of the life or work. But I've always distrusted this argument, and not liked it—nor liked Yeats much for giving voice to it—for it is not simply easy and specious, it is actually dangerous. No one in this or any other world has ever needed an excuse for being envious, mean, churlish, or arrogant.

And yet, Yeats was a very great poet, and evidently—measured by celebrity standards—not an awfully hard fellow to get along with, as a rule. Furthermore, most people argue that it is irrelevant what sort of person a writer is. In fact, there is some evidence that artists are more likely to be respected if they are a bit difficult—a bit tyrannical, selfish, nasty, and vicious.

Faulkner is reported to have said, in response to a poet's wretched treatment of his own mother, that "The Ode to a Grecian Urn" was worth any number of old ladies. But that is a badly flawed statement, for it is based upon an inconceivable—and ultimately irrelevant—hypothesis; and I would like to give Faulkner the benefit of the doubt and suppose he was sick, bilious, and mumbling drunk when he said it. But even to the extent that such an equation might seem to make sense, I believe that Keats himself would have despised it, for the evidence is that Keats was as amiable, sensitive, and kindly a young man as one is ever likely to encounter, in or out of literary circles . . . even though *Life Magazine* probably wouldn't have thought much of him.

Maybe he just didn't live long enough to become famous and vicious.

❦ My collecting of Hemingway's first editions during those first decades was active, though somewhat casual and haphazard. That is, I picked up every good buy I came upon, and these were of a considerable number, since Hemingway was sufficiently famous during most of his career for new titles of his books to be printed in great numbers. He was not only a respected and "literary" author, he was a popular one, whose books sold high in the thousands and were evidently read by great teeming populations of people who were not in themselves writers or critics, but simply honest, interested readers. He is, as the expression goes, fun to collect.

For example, eight or ten years ago, while going through a dealer's stock in Cleveland, I came upon a first-edition copy of *Winner Take Nothing* (N.Y., 1933) in dust jacket for $75.00. While the dj was torn at the edges, I thought this a very good price, and bought it. When I brought it home and compared it with my own first-edition copy (without the dust jacket), it impressed me as being not quite as bright a copy, so I removed the dj of the recently purchased copy and put it on my "original" first edition.

Then, I sent the second copy to the California Auction Gallery in San Francisco, where, lo and behold, it fetched $300 at auction!

Hey, this was fun! Then, within a few months, as it often happens, I found and bought another first-edition copy of *Winner Take Nothing*, this one *without* dj, but in equally fine condition and proportionately low in price, and shot it off to California, with the hope that I might collect another $300 for my alertness and industry. But such was not the case. This second copy sold for only $35.00—about as far beneath the theoretical value of the book without dj as $300 was above it.[1]

Now, in view of these shenanigans, who can say that the rare book market is not exciting? Truly, it is frolicsome and adventurous. It is a barrel of monkeys. Or mongeese. Or moneys. Choose your own, and why not—the bottom line being that it is not nearly so dependable, stable, and rationally governed as, say. . . well, the stock market.

❦　　　Recently, I came upon a major Hemingway title I had never—in spite of my modest Hemingway collection of first editions—possessed, nor even (shameful admission!) read; this was the inexpensive 1954 Scribner's reprint of *Green Hills of Africa*. When I began to read it, I could once more feel the old fascination, which has to do with the savoring of certain elemental, perhaps even "primitive," satisfactions. Here was a far different, far more generous book than *A Moveable Feast*. The mythic, legendary world that Hemingway inhabited was revealed through the noble simplicity of his language, which renders vivid and compelling all that is recorded.

The book's essential virtue is manifest in many places, in many ways, although all of these ways are immediately knowable. Here was the Hemingway I remembered, writing on one of his favorite subjects, hunting big game in Africa as it was done in the 1930's. *Green Hills* is novelistic, but not exactly a novel; it is a sort of *roman à clef*, in so far as it is a *roman* at all. It is a narrative of one of Hemingway's safaris, and the white hunters

---

1. Most rare book price guides tend to quote the higher figure and ignore the lower; this is why they sometimes prove misleading.

are all identifiable, although their names have been changed (except that he himself is referred to as "Hem"). The native Africans presumably bear their real-life names, which might suggest a sort of racism; but if it is, it's the "separate but equal" sort, for the Black guides and carriers are, within the narrow limitations of their roles, not without dignity and human interest.

The hunting party is an odd and interesting little microcosm, with trackers, guides, white hunters, a woman (Hemingway's, of course), and the little bureaucracy that such a hunting party inevitably becomes. Then, standing somewhere on the opposite side of the arena, and participating in a significantly different way, are the various sorts of big game: the rhinos, the water buffalo, the kudus, and the lions.

More interesting than the chase itself are the moments of leisure, usually at night before a campfire, when Hemingway and friends sit and talk about the strategies of the hunt, as well as about writing, warfare, morality, and life—with the night sounds of the bush providing atmosphere.

"By the fire, with whiskey and soda, we talked and I told them about it all." This sentence occurs near the end of the book; but for the reader, the ceremony is by now familiar. Man may be naturally a hunting animal; but he is surely a story-telling animal, as well. And no one can say whether the instinct for the hunt or for the tale is primary, for in Hemingway's world, neither is conceivable without the other—and such is this world's glory.

The magic is all here, very much as remembered. There are palpable satisfactions in *Green Hills*, and all praise is due to the man who wrote it. Still, it is a human production, after all: and there are flaws in the writing that I had either not noticed years ago when I'd read other Hemingway titles, or had simply dismissed as unimportant. Most surprising, perhaps, is the shakiness of Pappa's grammar. I take grammar seriously, aware of how much confusion and misunderstanding can arise from the neglect or abuse of its proprieties. And all along I had thought Hemingway felt the same way.

His dialogue, especially, is riddled with sophisticated hyper corrections. He has people always saying things like: "I feel badly." Maybe Hemingway was having fun with his characters, mocking them by having them speak such silliness; but I doubt it. Certainly he had nothing to gain by writing the following [p. 128, op. cit]: " . . . left the motor car standing there, and, Karl taking Charo and I, M'Cola to carry shells and birds, we agreed to work one on one side and one on the other side of the marsh."

Well, picky, picky. Mark Twain loses himself in a briarpatch of Missouri dialects, Henry James fastidiously blithers, and Homer nods. Fitzgerald consistently misspells Hemingway's name, even in letters to him (this may help explain some of that nasty business in *A Moveable Feast*), bringing to mind "Sockless Jerry Simpson," an old-time congressman from Medicine Lodge, Kansas, who, when caught in the act of misspelling the name of his own district, admitted as much, and claimed he had nothing but contempt for a man who couldn't spell the same word in more than one way.

So it is perhaps not a grievous sin that Hemingway falls asleep now and then in the midst of a sentence, and fails to play the grammar game according to the rules; still, his errors would be more easily forgiven if he had not so often behaved as one who knew all there is to know about good writing.

And yet, we would not respect him if he had not felt the magnitude of the writer's calling. To hear him tell it, there is nothing more important than "getting it down right." This means using language with clarity and verve, and it is aimed toward those beautiful, luminous precisions that are more than what is usually meant by "style," for it brightens the world around us, and is therefore a mighty ideal. He himself believed in it, and was aware of how many pitfalls there are in the writer's path. This is what much of *Green Hills of Africa* is about, for the difficulties in tracking big game and the difficulties of writing well are, like hunting and telling stories, intimately connected.

Indeed, the challenge is a great one, and, although it has to do with one's own ideals in writing well, it also has to do with public relations, publicity, and fame with all its consequences; it has to do with the game of literary reputations, which can never prove satisfying for anyone for very long. "Writers," he proclaims, scarcely one-fourth of the way into the book, "are forged in injustice as a sword is forged."

This is grandiose, to be sure, and one might wonder what right this famous author had to speak of injustice; but, of course there's always plenty to go around; and some find it more easily than others. So much is acceptable, even when it is rooted in grumpy resentment and self-conceit; after all, it extends to an ideal; and ideals do not exist anywhere but in the mind, even though we sometimes yearn for them to be palpable and real, as solid as water buffalo or high-powered rifles.

"What I had to do was work," he continues in the next paragraph. "I did not care, particularly, how it all came out. I did not take my own life seriously any more, any one else's life, yes, but not mine. They all wanted something I did not want and I would get it without wanting it, if I worked. To work was the only thing, it was the one thing that always made you feel good, and in the meantime it was my own damned life and I would lead it where and how I pleased."

This is not, perhaps, utterly devoid of fustian. The penultimate sentence, having to do with what "they" wanted and Hemingway did not, surely refers to fame . . . and even though at this time, in this mood, Hemingway may not have given a damn for fame, there were plenty of other times when he behaved as if nothing else was of much consequence.

The solecisms and hypocrises in *Green Hills of Africa,* however, are not nearly so embarrassing as the ridiculous posturing of his *Life Magazine* period, when our hero would speak of Marlene Dietrich as "the Kraut," and dated Ava Gardner, and rated his women like cattle or horses ("The Kraut was best"), and idolized Spanish bullfighters, who were presumed to have a special insight into life and death because they looked woeful and dressed in colorful tights and showed such things as grace under pressure.

Well, maybe this is unkind; and no doubt it is unfair to bullfighters; but I do not think it is unfair to the man who possessed such hubristic arrogance of popularity and flaunted it and began to feel that he could do no wrong, since photographers were there to catch him at it, whatever it might be, and worshipful journalists were waiting to translate it into heroic, if not grandiose, terms.

❦   All of this notwithstanding, and for all its faults, *Green Hills of Africa* is a remarkable book, one which could not have conceivably been written by anyone else. I have mentioned that it is a treatise on writing, in spite of its ostensible subject and locale, which is big-game hunting in Africa. But it is also something else; it is an odd variation upon that most popular of American *genres*—a sort of "How-to" book.

But a book on "how to what"? Well, partly, of course, how to conduct oneself in hunting big game in Africa. The book is not simply *about* big-game hunting, it's about the *aboutness*, about how it should be done. For each species, there is a unique method—a best way, to be sure—but also a sort of covenant. Pragmatism, ritual, and ethics intermingle, and even the issue of the morality of killing game for sport is raised.

Because of certain stereotyped notions (think of Wyndham Lewis' famous piece on Hemingway, titled "The Dumb Ox"), it is perhaps necessary, though a bit odd-sounding, to point out that Hemingway was, after all and in at least one important way, an extremely intelligent man; and for all his attentiveness to physical action and *thingness*, he did not live mindlessly. A reader of *Green Hills of Africa* must be aware that he did not hunt brutishly or avoid all consideration of the moral issue implicit in killing wild animals. One kills animals in obedience to instinct; and this instinct is good, if one understands it and abides by the rules. Even if one concedes that the rules are after all, and at least to some extent, man-made, they are rational and orderly, and within their jurisdiction, one may find pleasure and honor.

In reference to shooting game, along with his own wounds and injuries (more were to come later), Hemingway wrote: "I did nothing that had not been done to me." At first, this sounds a bit childish, and it is indeed a curious defense; but it is not a negligible one. It implies that both men and animals are players in a game whose rules are somewhat more than arbitrary, or even man-made; it implies that there is something more than a set of arbitrary and man-made rules, after all—there is a code that is natural, tacit, universal, and therefore inescapable. "The Short Happy Life of Francis Macomber" bears testimony to such a belief.

But there is more to learning how to live than in obeying the rules for hunting in Africa. The whole enterprise that absorbs the characters in *Green Hills of Africa* is the sort of rich man's game—especially as it was played in the 1930's—that reflects larger spheres of human activity in various ways. As with all good writing, the meanings generated by specific references go far beyond their minimal significance; for, if they did not, why would any reader but a sportsman ever be interested?

We live symbolically; and a clear and vivid account of what it is like to be on a month's hunting safari in Africa in the 1930's is necessarily about life itself, in all its forms. The hunt is therefore synecdoche of all human pursuits, and it is important that we should understand how it is done. Thus, the book is not simply about how to hunt big game on an African safari, or even about how to write; it is about how to live one's life.

🎝   *Green Hills of Africa* is divided into four parts and thirteen chapters. The chapters are untitled, but the parts are all given titles beginning with the word, "pursuit," as follows: "Pursuit and Conversation," "Pursuit Remembered," "Pursuit and Failure," and "Pursuit as Happiness."

If pursuit and happiness can be equated, then it follows that this must be a very happy book, for there is no section that does not partly bear that happy label. And, indeed, it is a happy book; it is touched by two sorts of magic: hope and myth. The hopefulness is implicit in the spirit of reckless pleasure. The freshness of possibility permeates the entire adventure, and even the occasional postures of cynicism and despair have a certain theatricality to them, for this pursuit, like most others, is radiant with promise.

It is the pursuit that matters; the goal is paradoxically achieved continually, if one understands the rituals implicit in means and ends:

> Finally the road began to lift gradually into the hills again, low, blue, wooded hills now, with miles of sparse bush, a little thicker than orchard bush, between, and ahead a pair of high, heavy, timbered hills that were big enough to be mountains. These were on each side of the road and as we climbed in the car where the red road narrowed there was a herd of hundreds of cattle ahead being driven down to the coast by Somali cattle buyers, the principle buyer walked ahead, tall, good-looking in white turban and coast clothing, carrying an umbrella as a symbol of authority.

Indeed, the things of this world are wonderful to behold and savor, and one's senses are a continuing miracle. Hemingway's ability to convey landscapes—a feel of distance, wind, sunlight, trees, and blowing grass—has never found a truer subject than in such epic arenas.

Contrasted with this great visual sweep are the felicities of humble detail. Hemingway's gifts are nowhere more evident than in the epiphanies of small insight . . . which, transformed by style, are revealed to be possessed of dimensions that have nothing to do with size.

Two examples will suffice: late one night after hours of whiskey and talk before the campfire, one of the hunters (named "Pop") has had a bit too much whiskey, and perhaps even enough talk, so he decides to retire. "He moved toward his tent carrying himself with comic dignity as though he were an open bottle."

This is tidy and precise enough; but there are better things. For example, it should be rememberd that in those years, before the development of relatively lightweight, high-velocity rifles that kill by shock rather than brute foot-poundage of impact, the most powerful guns—suitable for elephant, rhino, and water buffalo—were great heavy monstrous weapons, somwehat commensurate with the game they were designed to kill. Having wounded a buffalo, Hemingway discusses the possibility that it has been gut shot. The conversation is in whispers, and Hemingway quotes himself as follows: " 'The hell with that four-seventy,' I said. 'I can't shoot it. The trigger's like the last turn of the key opening a sardine can.' "

The heavy big-game cannons of the 1930's have been replaced by far more sophisticated weapons, and it is conceivable that there will come a time in human history when sardine cans will no longer exist . . . all of which will be a small pity, for then the wonderful tactile felicity of that simile will be lost.

❦   I have said that the book's happiness derives from two sorts of magic, hope and myth; and I have tried to suggest something of their presence in what has been written and quoted above. Hope and myth are essential for happiness; and their effect is magical. If small actions and long views are felt in certain ways, they convey a sense of promise, of imminence, of a world that constantly verges upon the marvelous, which is the natural habitat of myth.

What I am referring to is not simply a stylistic tick, it is a way of experiencing life. It is related to the capacities for wonder and pretense which are so natural to children when they play. If you are young enough, and if you are filled with the excitement of the felt imminence of immeasurable possibility, then, when you are talking about writing and literature, you can say anything—for what is there to limit the truth of what is possible? What Olympian utterances come naturally to mind, and how easily they can be spoken! "Some writers are only born to help another writer to write one sentence," Hemingway quotes himself early in the book, when he is in a pontificating mood.

But such nonsense doesn't matter, because there will always be more to say, and it doesn't make any real difference if what you say tomorrow evening around the campfire contradicts what you have said today. Talk about writing (which is, after all, talk about talk), along with talk about literature and morality and hunting, has to be just about the most interesting talk there is. Why, you can say anything, believing that somewhere (perhaps beyond some printed page) people will be listening very closely and will almost surely find it wise and good.

So, when Hemingway is in a grand and tragic mood, he says, "The hardest thing, because time is so short, is for [the writer] to survive to get his work done." Isn't it nice to be this young and this sure of things and this aware of how it is all done? Speaking of which, we mustn't forget the critics, "the lice who crawl on literature." Add that to the list, for literature is the greatest trophy of all, but we know what happens when those carcasses are left to lie in the brush too long. Nevertheless, say it and say it, and let's keep on talking.

Talk is essential, of course; but it's also raw material for writing. There is a truth to conversation, but there is a more abiding truth to the written word. *Verba volant, scripta manent,* the old Latin proverb states, and in your heart you know it is true—especially if you are a writer. Certainly, Hemingway knew it: "But you ought to always write it to try to get it stated. No matter what you do with it." This is not altogether unfamiliar, but it is mysticism, nevertheless. And as for propitiatory magic, we are told that [Hemingway's] " . . . temper has to go bad before he can write."

All of it is there, true and untrue and not quite either; but whatever its good sense or lack thereof, it is passionately focused upon the potential wonder and perfection of the text. The purpose of the safari may have been to kill big game, but for Hemingway it was to provide material for a book—any book, along with a few masterful short stories, depending upon how things turned out, and where that pursuit, which is happiness, led.

❦   It so happened that in one sense the safari ended after four sections, thirteen chapters, and 295 pages. It ended with the hopeful title, and motto, of that last section still justified: "Pursuit as Happiness."

So that is what the book is about. It is a how-to book about how to pursue things that are part of the wonder of this world. They do not have to loom large in any known scale of things; they can be discoveries as small and trivial as the feel of the trigger squeeze on an outmoded elephant rifle, or they can be as haphazard and silly as sitting in judgment upon matters that no one has ever had rightful authority to speak of.

You have to be young to believe these things; and so we add a third ingredient to hope and myth—youth. Maybe this last is the most important and the most comprehensive in that triad, subsuming the others. At that time, Africa seemed so vast, and the population of rhinos and elephants and water buffalo so great beyond counting, that one could kill them in a state approaching innocence; like literary truths, there would always be others to pursue. You could say it at the moment, relaxed and happy in the feeling it is profound and true, but knowing that there was plenty of time left to say other things, also, and they might not all agree. But so what? Let the carcasses lie there and collect critical vermin, because there is so much more awaiting us, whichever direction we might decide to take, out into that expanse that is all open, vast, exciting—like the Future, or like a great continent filled with big game, adventures without end, and at the end of every day, good whiskey and talk around the campfire.

The tragedy is that, like all pursuits, this one had to come to an end; and finally, it may have seemed that all the pursuits Hemingway could believe in were over, and all he had to say had been said. Thus, in the world he had claimed as his own—the only world he could understand, after all—there was really nothing new that was left; he had run out of things to learn about or pursue; the old days of youth were gone, and the continent was tamed and the rifles were light and deadly and just about all the things you could say about writing and literature seemed to have been said. Also, he was an old man, which was something his great gifts could neither accommodate nor guard against. The Future no longer existed; it was already here. Therefore it was only logical—which is to say, in the nature of things—that the pursuit was over and the possibility for happiness had ended.

🍎 A Frontier Doctor

Last fall, as I write this, I attended a small estate auction in the southeastern Ohio village of Wellston, where approximately 1000 books were to be sold. When I arrived, I saw that the books were displayed far better than usual at such sales—they were conveniently placed spine-up in boxes upon trestle tables arranged end-to-end. Not all the boxes on the tables contained books, nor were all the boxes with books on the tables—some were underneath and others had been placed on the lawn parallel with the tables. They were lined up with old lawnmowers, rakes, vacuum cleaners, radios, and boxes of miscellaneous items—which is to say, junk.

Virtually all of the books were worn and dirty textbooks, hymnals, bookclub editions of once-popular novels, and similarly cheap and uninspiring reprints. But there was one book among them that promised to make it all worthwhile. As it happened, this was also the oldest, having been printed in 1815. Many books of that age are worthless; but the preponderance of worthless books among those from 1815 is, of course, far smaller than those printed a century later.

I remember this morning as showing southern Ohio autumn weather at its flamboyant best—sunny, but with a cool apple cider sharpness in the air. The smoky wooded hills bordering the Appalachian Highway on my drive to Wellston had all the tints of rusted iron, antique beaten copper, and gold. Even at noon, you could smell the imminence of frost that would creep into the dark swales of the cow pastures around midnight.

By the time I arrived at the house in Wellston, people were beginning to crowd around the tables, examining everything in sight; and the rich, warm odors of hot coffee and chili dogs emanated from the caterers in the garage. The thought of waiting for that single book to come up in the natural progression of the auction was not too dreary a prospect. Still, I would have to stand close enough to keep watch and make sure that someone didn't pluck it out and move it to another box.

The ethics of such a maneuver is problematic. No one likes to wait for two or three hours, then bid on a particular box with the assumption that it contains a coveted title, only to find upon getting it that the book is no longer there. Surprise! Somebody has moved that book to another box, or possibly into a pocket or purse; but I don't think *this* happens often, and it is best not dwelt upon. Obviously, one should keep an eye on the specific box or boxes where the good stuff is.

Is this too much to ask? Well, yes and no. Although sneaky, last-minute shifting is opprobrious, verging upon the sinister, no reasonable book person will object to someone gathering a set together when the volumes that make it up have been distributed willy-nilly throughout several boxes. A set whose volumes are randomly distributed lacks integrity in the literal sense. Why should you have to bid on odd volumes of a broken set repeatedly until you own the whole thing? Because of a book or books you have no interest in, you might have to spend more for the last volume in, say, the sixth box, than you would have been willing to pay for the entire set.

Not only that, how did the set get scattered to begin with? The auctioneers' helpers (seldom guilty of literary or scholarly scrupulousness) grab the books up as they can and stuff them into boxes. No one will blame them for this, because they simply don't know any better—and one reason they don't know any better is that books at this sort of auction don't generally bring enough for these folks to worry about keeping them together. Not only that, the books may have been packed miscellaneously, and the sets scattered, long before these helpers came upon the scene.

The specific problem with sets demonstrates a more general truth, that in an estate auction there is nothing to suggest that the distribution of titles in a box has been selected, let alone ordained, by God. Why shouldn't the collector, the potential buyer, have as much to say about the distribution of books as a totally uninterested heir or auctioneer's helper? Therefore, if you see half a dozen titles you would like to bid on—even if they aren't parts of a set—why should you be expected to wait and bid upon them as they are casually distributed in, say, four boxes, so that in bidding for each box you will be bidding mostly for titles you don't want, but competing for books which others may covet, eager to pay a high price and drive the bid skyward?

That is a long question, and these are difficult matters to think reasonably upon. They represent a genuine conflict of interest, which partakes more of mercantile convention than of ethical conduct, for even if you take matters in your own hands and rearrange books to suit your own interests, others have the right to look them over. And if you and another buyer cannot agree upon the composition of titles in a particular box, then the titles should be auctioned off individually, sold to the highest bidder. Auctioneers should not object to this, for it is tangible evidence that a particular book deserves to be sold at some sort of premium. And auctioneers of estates need all the help they can get, because they don't know good books from door nails or tulip bulbs.

❦   So on this day I decided to do the safe and proper thing: I plucked out the one title I was interested in, took it up to the auctioneer, and asked him to sell it separately. He agreed, and put it on the shelf of the small table he was going to use. He and the table were on a platform, so that it was convenient for me to keep watch over the book and come fully awake when he'd finished with the glassware, china, and various assortments of knick-knacks that seem—for reasons I will never understand—to attract most interest in such places.

Eventually the auctioneer came to "my" book and asked for an opening bid of five dollars, glancing in my direction. I opened the bid, of course. If you ask for a book to be put up especially, you are expected to open the bid; and this is only just and reasonable.

But then my bid was quickly raised by an antique dealer friend, a woman from Middleport, Ohio. She specializes in antique furniture and is not interested in books, knowing little about them; but I was not entirely surprised that she should perk up at the sight of this one. The bid rose swiftly to twenty dollars, and then slowed abruptly. My friend knew the book had to be interesting; but as a dealer, she was aware that this was simply not in her line, so she hesitated, then, finally, remained silent, whereupon the book was knocked down to me for $22.50. The fact is, I would have gone to a hundred; but naturally I am pleased that I wasn't forced to go that high. And it is the occasional bargain that keeps one showing up at country and small town estate auctions where the chances of encountering the exceptional item are . . . well, *exceptional.*

As for the book itself: it was small, bound in old calf, and somewhat warped and battered. I had never heard of either the book or the author. And, while 1815 is very old for most things, it is practically yesterday in the context of books. But age, like many things in this world, is a relative matter. According to the old belief, Adam was created at the age of thirty, which is young in most contexts, but old for a senior in high school. And while an 1815 imprint would not be of the least *antiquarian* interest if printed in New York, Philadelphia or Boston, it is respectably old for Frankfort, Kentucky, where this book was printed. As for its author and title, they are listed on the title page as follows:

Valuable Vegetable
MEDICAL
PRESCRIPTIONS,
FOR THE CURE OF ALL
NERVOUS AND PUTRID
DISORDERS.
BY DOCTOR RICHARD CARTER
FRANKFORT, (KEN.)
1815

I have omitted part of this title page. Directly beneath "Disorders" there is the passage from Proverbs (10, 27), stating that, "The Fear of the Lord prolongeth days," followed by a brief commentary. Then, at the bottom of the page, directly above the date of publication, exactly where it should be, are the names "Gerard & Berry—Printers to the Commonwealth."

Collectors of old books will not be deceived: here is a book that possesses many of the qualities of an "herbal"—a rare and most collectible sort of book whose quaintness and interest tend to increase in direct proportion to age. And for Frankfort, Kentucky, this book is old enough to have some status as a primitive, if not antiquarian, object. Furthermore, its age is such that it is interesting in ways that would be of little professional comfort to "Doctor" Richard Carter, if he were alive today and could be apprised of the fact.

Shortly after they are published, medical books, like their legal cousins, fall into a limbo in which they are too old to be relevant but not old enough to be interesting. What is the duration in years of this limbo? Well, it depends. Subscribers to certain types of legal reference works are periodically supplied with addenda as new laws are enacted and new decisions alter the ceremony of precedence, so that an updated book ten or fifteen years old may be as useful as if it were just published—which would clearly not be the case with a text on physiology of similar age . . . assuming that physiological tomes cannot be as conveniently updated in a similar manner.

Regarding medical books, one of the factors of obsolescence is that of the exponential increase in medical technology (similar to that of technology generally), so that the majority of those medical books affected by growth in chemical and electronic (e.g., laser surgery) sophistication are rendered obsolete with a sometimes bewildering swiftness. Books on anatomy, however, tend to retain their usefulness far longer, because significant advances in the study of anatomy do not occur with such frequency.[1]

Given the rapid advances in medicine, texts of only a century before often retain and reflect ideas that seem quaint to us. And if there is an 1815 medical book whose nostrums derive largely from plants in nature, rather than from their synthetic laboratory progeny and simulacra . . . especially if the text is afflicted with culture lag, which is to say, if it was written on the frontier by a self-educated (i.e., ignorant) physician . . . then, if your tastes run to the gaudier varieties of human error, you are in for such a feast of quaint and curious folklore that you will emerge from it filled with wonder that anybody could have ever, under any circumstances, survived such cures.

But, of course, many didn't survive such cures at all; they died in spite of them, or were killed by them. Seldom has sheer, dumb mortality flourished as it did on the frontier. If all of our ancestors who died before the age of twenty had died only a year younger, none of us would be here to contemplate the fact.

1. Henry Gray's *Anatomy*, first published in 1858, had gone through sixteen editions by 1911, as reported in the *Encyclopaedia Britannica's* 11th edition. Somewhat modified, it remained a classic textbook well into the twentieth century. It is curious that while this fact is reported in the Britannica entry under "Anatomy," there is no biographical entry for Henry Gray himself.

🍂   Although Richard Carter's book is a most bizarre and extraordinary production, it begins soberly enough. The author describes a world that is an arena of Manichaean strife between good and evil—with industry good, and sloth evil. The moral cast of his Preface is so great, one might quickly and easily forget that this is ostensibly the entry into a medical text:

> We young gentlemen, will talk about the system that strengthens the
> nerves, and purifies the blood: It is divine industry, queen mother of
> all our virtues, and of all our blessings; what is there great or good
> in this wide world, that springs not from thy royal bounty? And thou
> infernal sloth, fruitful fountain of all our crimes, what is there mean
> or miserable in the lot of man, that flows not from thy hellish malice?

The moral is inescapably clear: the harder you work, the healthier you become. Or stay. Or something. And there is much more of this, with frequent reliance upon Scripture and liberal use of anecdote. And all of this is still in the Preface, even before the Introduction, not to mention the opening chapters, which are titled, "The Dysentery, or Bloody Flux" and "The Cholera Morbus, or Purging and Vomiting."

What were Carter's credentials? What was required to be a physician on the frontier in Kentucky? Well, *testimonials*. And Carter provides a rich sampling, even before we have gotten to the homily on hard work. The first three that follow are in sequence on pages viii and ix:

> I do certify that I had a cancer about five or six years past on my nose,
> it increased fast, and spread over my face in places, till I went to
> doctor Richard Carter, he began to doctor me, and I think it is now
> sound and well, from its appearance. Given under my hand, this 29th
> of September, 1812.
>
>   Wm. Embry
>
>   Test,
> Wm Embry
> Moses Swinney

> I do certify that I had as severe convulsion fits as ever a person had
> to live: I would be gone for the space of an hour and a half that they

could not observe breath, and a half dozen could not open my hands, without breaking them. Doctor Richard Carter tended on me, and from last fall, till now, I have been clear of them. Given under my hand, the 30th of September, 1812—Paint Lick, Garrard county.

Mary Ann Coy

Test,
Jacob Maxey
Moses Swinney
Isaac Embry

Garrard county, at the mouth of Paint Lick. I do certify that I had a negro fellow, that was down with the galloping consumption, that he was past all hopes, (apparently); he coughed and spit vastly, and had to be turned in bed. Doctor Richard Carter attended him, he mended greatly in a short time; and is now sound and well.

David Reynolds

Test,
Henry Reynolds, Sr.
Henry Reynolds, Jr.

Then there is the following testimonial, which is edifying because of its reference to a woman physician, "a doctress woman":

Sarah M'Afee, on Drake's Creek—I was taken in child bed; had been in a low state a long time, and Dr. Richard Carter, brought on deliverance; attended me till I recovered, more than I ever expected by a doctor. I had been under a Doctress woman twelve months.

SARAH M'AFEE

These testimonials are interesting for various reasons, not the least of which is the industry of the Swinney and Embry clans in testifying on medical matters. Especially noteworthy is the testimony of William Embry regarding the truthfulness of his own testimony. Unless that was, indeed, another "William Embry"—which fact should have been noted, one would think, in case there were those among the sick and the lame who took their texts seriously and carefully read what was before them.

I have gone from the book's opening pages back to the preface, and now—to sustain this retrograde motion—I will go back even farther, to within one leaf of the title itself. Here we have the "Advertisement," which in 1815 meant something significantly different from what it means now. Then, long before medial institutionalization, the word meant simply a notice, or—as the etymology informs us—any advertising, or "turning of the mind," towards something.

The Advertisement for Carter's book reads as follows:

RICHARD CARTER, The son of Richard Carter, was born in the year of our Lord, 1786, July the 27th, and had a sister by the name of Lynda Carter, was born February the 22nd, 1792. I was born on the south branch of the Potomac, and was educated in Virginia; my father was of the English descent, and my mother of the Indian. I have a family of my own, and being a stranger in this country, and much exposed, I have got a few to set down their cures, that with the help of God I have done for them: Not being a regular bred doctor, but mostly by herbs, barks, root's, &c.

As the most of this performance is intended for the poor, and such as cannot conveniently obtain the aid of physicians, at particular times, I have taken the liberty to substitute my own prescriptions, for the cure of such particular complaints as have frequently fallen under my own observation and management. I feel conscious of benevolent intentions, whatever be the reception of this work.

RICHARD CARTER

A most curious business, indeed! What is his sister, Lynda, doing here? Was she famous in her own right? Is there some occult relevance denied to those of us today? Well, we'll never know. Richard Carter's prose is scarcely more clear-headed than his medicine, as documented by the text that follows.

But we haven't yet quite exhausted the mystery of the Advertisement, which reveals that exasperating habit of so many early commentators in referring to Indians of all sorts simply as "Indians," without any tribal designation whatsoever, as if they were, indeed, all alike—when in reality their cultures were almost as various as those of all the nations of Europe. And here the reference is to his own *mother*, who was evidently just an "Indian" like all the others!

But if Indians were viewed as pretty much all alike, and in this way dehumanized, their image, as we would say today, was not altogether unworthy. Although the appearance and behavior of many tribes were ostentatiously unChristian and demonic (almost literally embodying the visions of devils that had lurked in the European imagination since the Middle Ages), they were nevertheless often believed to be possessed of uncanny powers, which, in that day of cups and leeches, was identified with the general mystery of healing. Thus it is that Richard Carter somewhat proudly displays his Indian heritage, hinting at the dark arts of herbal healing (certainly far beyond the skills of European medicine), rooted as they were in the deep mysteries of roots themselves, along with barks, berries, herbs, and the body parts of animals. Here, the reference is to ancient, primitive tribal lore—the wisdom of untold generations, as employed by medicine men and healing women.

Given the crude diagnostic strategies of those days, even the list of ailments strikes us as curious. What is the modern reader to make of "The Nervous Cholic, or Wind in the Blood," "The Negro Poison," and "The Cold Fever, or Tiger Gripe"? Carter boasts that in the year 1813 he lost only two out of sixty-seven patients to the last-mentioned—but the reader can't help but wonder if it might not have been a theoretically non-fatal disease, even in those days.

Evidently it was a new one, for Carter states that it "has been approaching through the land since the shaking of the earth, and is little understood, though many opinions have been drawn upon it." His reference to the "shaking of the earth" is to the great forty-day earthquake of 1811 and 1812, which changed the course of the Mississippi River and formed Reelfoot Lake. Kentuckians would have been well-aware of this vast turbulence, for it was a catastrophe of Biblical proportions and western Kentuckians lived near its center.

Carter seems to connect the rise of Tiger Gripe with the great earthquake, and the contemplation of the two of them together throws him into a state of awful humility. He is abashed and mystified, and before he can get down to the business of describing symptoms, he falls into an eschatological fit and speaks darkly of thunder, lightning, sulphur, and charges of gun powder.

But after a full page of general incoherence, he finally gets down to the matter at hand, which is to say, The Cold Fever or Tiger Gripe:

The symptoms of this complaint are violent, and if not early checked soon set all medicine aside. It often comes with cold chills, then a high fever, a pain in the side, (sometimes in the right, sometimes in the left), it is most fatal when in the left; pain in the head, an aching in the bones; sickness at the stomach. If there be sickness at the stomach, a puke is necesary (of ipecacuanha); if in the bowels, a purge of calomel; then a miraculous sweat: Get a pint of whiskey, heat it boiling hot, set it on fire, put the still cap over it, and put the little end in the bed, as hot as the patient can bear the steam.—Where the pain is most acute, cup, scarify and blister; but by no means let blood; draw blisters on the chest; boil red pepper, mustard seed, salt petre and whiskey together, and wash where the pains are most severe. If the head ache is acute, beat peech tree bark, and wet it in good strong vinegar, and bind to the forehead; or fetherfew and vinegar; snuff the juice of groundivy, or harts-horn; bind roasted poke roots to the soles of the feet. Bathe the feet in weak lye; apply a blister behind each ear, and the back of the neck. If the pain still continues in the head, shave a large place on the top and apply a plaster there. If the cough is hard, get a handful of horehound, a handful of spikenar, a handful of the bark of the root of spicewood, a handful of allecompain, a handful of comfrey, a handful of the bark of the root of yellow poplar, boil them in three gallons of water to one, strain it; add a quart of honey, a quart of hard cider, a table spoonful of salt-petre, a table spoonful of dried Indian turnip, boil them to a quart; take from a half a spoonful three times a day, to a spoonful three times a day, and keep the bowels open with purging salts, castor-oil, cream of tartar and the like.

There is more of this sort of gnarled poetry, with a few more instruments added to the score (sycamore chips, rye meal, and catnip, for example), but you get the idea. And that idea is not very pleasant to contemplate. It is a wonder that anyone survived the cure, which Carter himself may have suspected, for he rather abruptly and surprisingly ends this particular entry with the following quattrain in purest doggerel:

> When Doctors first began their skill,
> A many a patient they did kill;
> But now they've got it in possession,
> They give the means, and say, God bless them.

Another odd disease, or condition, is referred to simply as "jaw fall." What is it? Carter states that it is a disease of young children, then adds breezily that, "The name is sufficiently expressive of its nature." I personally don't find this true, although it suggests a somewhat adenoidal expression. But this is hard to think of as an ailment, precisely, and still harder to imagine as an affliction among infants, who seem, in this account, to be the primary victims. "I think it seldom occurs in this country," he continues "but whenever it does happen, it is said to be incurable; it may be prevented, however, by purging the child soon after its birth with the following preparation . . . ." Then follows a prescription as promised.

The confusion here is impressive; in fact, it approaches the marvelous. Note how the words "I think" and "it is said to be" remove Carter from intimate acquaintance with the disease; then note how confidently he offers a preventive. The rarity of the affliction does not help matters at all, and the entry reminds one of that old joke that has a man going through some extravagant series of gestures "to keep the elephants away"—and when he is told indignantly that he's being ridiculous, because there aren't any elephants anywhere near, he says triumphantly, "See?"

The crudity of some of these old cures verges upon the loathsome, no doubt reinforcing some fundamentalist instinct for guilt and suffering in the name of original, or perhaps subsequent, sin. "To Dry Up The Milk in a Woman's Breast" is given an entry almost as brief as the title; but it is nevertheless too long. "Take the stinking mud from the kitchen door, where dish or slop water is thrown out, heat it and put it to the breast as a poultice." That's all, but it is certainly more than enough; and I would like to think that the "doctress woman" referred to earlier would not have prescribed so gross a remedy.

There is much more, of course; and there are diseases that are still recognizable by name, if not necessarily by diagnosis. (The section on cancer is memorable, but I'll forego it here.) And the variety of humble, frontier herbs and potions is as rich an assortment as you could imagine, even with a high fever. Carter's prescription for pluerisy alone contains such folklore curiosities as squirrel broth, rye mush, buttermilk, Seneca (spelled "sennaca") snake root, nettles, brimstone, eggs, sulphur, roasted apples or currants, vinegar, a quart of rye whiskey, beat rattle snake root (whatever that is), dried cat dung, butterfly roots, pokeberries, and sawdust of light wood. There is even more, and the mixtures and alternatives are not without interest; but I will resist the urge to list them.

Carter ends with an Index, which seems arbitrarily logical in such a book; but there it is, for all to see. Now, in the approach to my own ending, I'll repeat the retrograde motion of my beginning, and state that before the Index, there is a glossary of medical terms. In this, an occasional surprise is encountered, but nothing of major importance. The word "manual" is spelled "manuel," and defined as "Performed by the Hand." This is largely correct, and is not deserving of our contempt. Nor is the listing of "Indigestion" great cause for mirth; it is defined as "A disease in which the food lies heavy and unchanged in the stomach." Although we might not dignify it with the label "disease" in this enlightened time, we can recognize the condition—for it has lain heavy and unchanged for these near-200 years since Carter's book was published.

Immediately before the Glossary are three pages of poetry, properly unsigned and no doubt the work of Carter himself. He just couldn't seem to get stopped, which is a pity, I suppose—although the verse is certainly no more wretched than what he would have called "the physic." One of these poems is a retelling in verse of the fable concerning the grasshopper and the ant; and we are reminded of Carter's prolegomenon on industry and sloth. The last poem, however, gives a description of the "Great Chain of Being" that would have been recognizable to Professor Lovejoy himself:

> Each creature is link'd to that below it;
> All nature, if observ'd, will show it,
> And upwards stil our search will prove,
> Each link'd again to that above.
> Heaven, when it had created man,
> Unfinish'd saw creation's plan;
> Nor would the links together meet
> Until woman did the chain complete.

Immediately before this, in the book's reluctant departure from the reader's attention, are the Twelve Signs of the Zodiac, followed by Carter's brief commentaries on their "nature." Here we find that some months are good for bleeding (Libra and Saggittarius), some indifferent (Cancer and Pisces), and some evil (Taurus and Leo).

"No man ought," Carter concludes, "to make incissions, nor touch with iron, the members governed by any sign the day that the moon is in it, for fear of the great effusion of blood that may happen. Nor when the sun is in it, for fear of the great danger and peril that might follow therefrom."

With this final warning, I will also end my piece, leaving you to wonder what I have necessarily omitted. There is little likelihood that you will ever know what Doctor Carter thought about Warts on the tongue, the Falling Down of the Lower Intestines, or The King's Evil. But you may be sure that your health will not suffer; nor do I think your days on earth will be shortened or impoverished due to such ignorance.

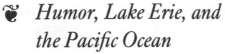# Humor, Lake Erie, and
the Pacific Ocean

R ecently I was invited to Saddleback College, in
Orange County, California, to attend a chamber theater production of a play that had been
adapted from my novel, *Sassafras*. It was a
pleasant visit, and personally interesting for several reasons, one of which
must be familiar to every novelist whose work has been made into a film
or play. I speak of seeing my characters represented, if not embodied, by
living actors. I watched them behave in oddly familiar ways and speak
sentences that I had first heard uttered in the silence and dark privacy of
my imagination.

During this visit I stayed in Laguna Beach, in a motel room that directly
overlooked the Pacific Ocean. On the washstand lay two light gilt coins
with "No Cash Value" printed on one side, and "Freedom" on the other.
I assumed they were welcome tokens for the guests, so I pocketed them.
The next morning, two more appeared, which I pocketed. And, on the
third morning, the same. I reckoned that if I stayed there long enough, I
might get wealthy, except for the fact that . . . well, these little coins had
no cash value. Precisely as stated.

At high tide, I could almost have jumped from the balcony at the
back of my room into the foamy reaches of the surf, although it would
have been a long jump and a hard landing. Awaking in the morning,
I looked out upon the ocean—that great breezy pulsatile creature—and
listened to the breakers. The weather was bright and sunny, attended
by obstreperous seagulls drifting in the air—just as it always should be
in such places; and there were even some theatrical dolphins parading
up and down a mere hundred yards offshore. I was really being given
the treatment.

Anyone who has just lived through the cold dank basement of an Ohio
winter would appreciate such a setting, but I liked it for an additional

reason. Although I had looked out upon the Pacific Ocean a number of times, in various places, this was the first time I had seen it since reading W. R. Burnett's *High Sierra*, in which the protagonist—a man named Roy who is also from Ohio—first gazes upon it and utters a line that I'll never forget. Burnett records the moment as follows: " 'So that's the Pacific Ocean,' said Roy. 'I'll take Lake Erie.' "[1]

I have not quoted that directly from the text, but I am certain of its correctness (surely a modest boast of mnemonic accomplishment), and I find the utterance sadly hilarious, as well as a bit uncanny. I have often thought of Roy's words. I am aware of the possibility that I am alone in my mirth. I know that I may find this sentence funnier than just about anyone else would find it, but I can't help myself. Although the joke may, indeed, be a somewhat private one, or perhaps limited and regional (those of us who are regionally underprivileged never fully believe this deep in our hearts, of course), its humor is nevertheless intrinsic to it. That is to say, no matter how one might judge the quality of the humor, no one could question that the humor is there.

But exactly *how* is it humorous? This is a question that has been asked many times in many different contexts; and it is almost always pointed toward a general definition of humor. The fact that this question has so often been asked indicates that it is obviously worth asking. It isn't the kind of question that leads to only one sort of answer; it leads into all sorts of inscrutable complexities. But then, it is possible that such polysemic resourcefulness is indicative of its genius. There are, after all, those sorts of questions that require precise, categorical answers for transactional completion and semantic integrity; and then there are those other sorts of questions that are ruined by answers. Or *would* be ruined, if adequate, definitive answers were ever available.

But in the present context, I will be content with a lesser, more manageable question. What precisely is it that happens in this statement which brings Roy, the Pacific Ocean, and Lake Erie together in a strange and interesting context? Although we are in the presence of mystery, here, we

1. Most people will know Roy best as the character played by Humphrey Bogart in the film, *High Sierra*; although I can't remember that he actually speaks the sentence quoted.

are not without answers at all. In fact, several answers are available, and it seems to me that all are obvious, important, and interesting. The least important, is the fact that this "overheard" comment of Roy's comes unexpectedly, in an entirely unlikely context, surprising the reader. One isn't prepared for it, which makes it all the more remarkable, since most humorous effects depend upon some sort of preparation or staging that enables us to feel that the humor is shared, or at least sharable. Like all communications, humor is to some extent conventional and appropriate. Even in unexpected comic intrusions, there is likely to be some vantage point ready for mounting, from which we can view the action and know that it is appropriate to laugh.

And yet one can read *High Sierra* from beginning to end and not laugh once (not even at what I have written, for it is really more humorous than laughable). *High Sierra* is simply not in any way a funny book. It is far from it; it is a tragic book. I have written elsewhere[1] about Burnett and his undeserved neglect as a writer, along with how I "discovered" him by coming upon a copy of the bound galleys of *High Sierra* at a book sale, buying it, and reading a library copy of the novel (to preserve my copy's freshness) with an immediate sense of pleasure and awakening.

Nor is there anything mysterious about another aspect of the humor in Roy's pronouncement, for it is immediately recognizable—it belongs to that venerable tradition of the rural comic bumpkin, whose sturdy ignorance is proof against virtually all the world. Through this tradition, it partakes of regional humor, which is one of the enduring strains in American culture; and the insular cast of mind finds natural expression in such bathos. One of its memorable instances is Mark Twain's reported comment upon first seeing Niagara Falls: "I pronounce it a great success."

And yet there is more than buffoonery at work in Roy's remark Salinity, surf, and tide excepted—Lake Erie presents as vast a prospect as the Pacific Ocean. One cannot "see across" Lake Erie any more than one can see across the Pacific Ocean, and not being able to see across something is a phenomenal absolute. There are no degrees to it; if a body of water is too vast to see across, then it is a large body of water, and that's that. Maps of the world may convey to us the great discrepancy in size between the second smallest Great

---

1. *Booking in the Heartland.* Johns Hopkins, 1986.

Lake and the world's vastest ocean, but this is abstract knowledge—which is to say, it is essentially the mind, not the eye, that informs us of this fact.

Such reflections bring vividly to mind my first glimpse of Lake Erie. My parents, sister, and I were visiting the resort of Cedar Point, at Sandusky, Ohio. This was probably in the summer of 1929 or 1930, sometime near my fourth or fifth birthday. I will never forget that first sight of water—hazy, vast, and distant—that affected me so powerfully. I remember that the sight "took my breath away"; and this expression, though hackneyed, nevertheless expresses exactly what I felt. Or, it expresses what I feel I felt—but that's good enough, for all memories are mediated and therefore subject to such impurities of access.

This memory is one of my earliest, and it has stayed with me loyally. As low and gentle as the "surf" of Lake Erie is, it was nevertheless sufficient to knock me down and give me a noseful of water. I cried out for my daddy, and then just settled down and cried. It was an interesting experience, and I remember that my parents and sister thought my being knocked down by a wave was all good fun, so eventually I learned to think so, too.

Then, some four and a half decades later, I was enabled to see Lake Erie from an entirely different perspective, and it changed my sense of one of the first absolutes I had ever experienced. I was on a commercial night flight from Detroit to Cleveland, after traveling to Kalamazoo, Michigan, to appraise an estate library. I looked out the window to my left and saw a large grid of bright lights, which must have been Leamington, Ontario; then, I looked out the the window to the right and saw clusters of lights that must have shone from the archipelago formed by the Bass Islands and Put In Bay. Then, in the far distance beyond those lights, dense bright clusters that were probably Sandusky and Cedar Point.

What had happened to that wonderful sense of being on the edge of some boundless realm? Where was that great, hazy, looming horizon of water? Lake Erie, which had taken my breath away almost fifty years before, now gave it back to me; and part of my sense of the vastness and wonder of the world was diminished.

🦋 I have not forgotten Roy as he first views the Pacific Ocean in his moment of mild surmise. And, to be sure, with that expression we reach an enormous distance, from Keats' sonnet, "On First Looking Into Chapman's Homer," to Roy muttering a prosaic assessment at the indifferent expanse before him.

Although Keats' poem is so famous it may seem unnecessary to quote from it, I will nevertheless do so for purposes of contrast. The poem, you will remember, requires that we think of Chapman's translation of Homer from the original Greek as analogous to the reports of those first great explorers who had gazed upon new worlds. Implicit, also, is the premise that imaginary worlds conveyed through the written word possess their own beauty, power, and reality. A great book is like a new world, and the reader enters it as a discoverer. In this case, the reader is escorted through that wondrous realm by one who speaks both languages, as it were: that of the natives and that of the visitor, so that he can explain and translate all. But this particular tour guide passes on more than information; he passes on his own function, as well, so that Keats, the reader, marvels at how reading this mighty work has transformed him:

> Then felt I like some watcher of the skies
> When a new planet swims into his ken;
> Or like stout Cortez when with eagle eyes
> He stared at the Pacific and all his men
> Look'd at each other with a wild surmise
> Silent, upon a peak in Darien.

It seems obvious that Roy, Burnett's ignorant and inarticulate protagonist didn't know anything by either Chapman or Keats; but then, in all fairness, it must be pointed out that no available evidence suggests that Keats knew a great deal about Lake Erie, even if his brother, George, did settle in Louisville, Kentucky, only two or three hundred miles away. Apparently, Keats didn't even know that it was Balboa, rather than Cortez, who had discovered the Pacific Ocean. Then again, maybe Keats did know this, but felt that "Balboa" would not have scanned well. He was right, although the line remains the weakest in the poem, so Cortez wasn't much help after all.

Nevertheless, we can conclude that the hero of W. R. Burnett's *High Sierra* and John Keats are different sorts of people. But who would have thought otherwise? Keats was all sensibility and eagerness; Roy was trapped, ignorant, and half-crazed by unrequited love. One was real and the other fictional. But as different as they were, both were *fey*—in the old sense of the word: they had a clear and accurate premonition that they would die young; and I am sure there must be some sort of lesson in that, although its full import eludes me at the moment.

Only one thing more need be said about Roy's utterance, and then we can leave him sneering at the Pacific Ocean, knowing that he will soon be shot to death somewhere high in the Sierra Mountains to the east. This is the wonderful whimsy in his observation. It is colored by what at first seems a beautiful nonsense. But even that nonsense is suggestive of a deeper connection, which has to do with Roy's homesickness throughout the novel. He is far from home, and even though—like most of Burnett's characters—he has little self-knowledge, in the wacky pronouncement he reveals what we would today call his "vulnerability"—his tragic sense of remoteness from all that is happy and good, his need to belong, his need to be loved by the girl he loves so much . . . and intermixed with all of these, a terrible and pathetic homesickness.

The only real home Roy has known was as a child in Ohio, and now, as a man who is cut off from the world and drifting, he looks upon the great and beautiful ocean with curious indifference, and compares it invidiously to "Ohio's" lake—as it is described in crossword puzzles—which he can identify as something now remote, but once near and familiar, to which he is connected by invisible bonds.

🎋   During my brief visit in Laguna Beach, I managed to do very little booking, but did find a bookstore of both new and used books, and in it came upon a first-edition copy of Sacheverell Sitwell's *Truffle Hunt*, London (1953), in somewhat tattered dj, and with both front fly leaves cropped. I don't usually find the Sitwells much to my taste (I bunch them all together, like carrots), but a quick glance through this particular book suggested that it might be interesting. For one thing, it consisted of short pieces that would not likely prove as tiring as I seem to remember all the Sitwell's longer texts being.

And so much was true. Not only that—since our present subject is humor—there are two excellent jokes in this book that are worth passing along. The first makes use of the sort of typographical error that seems the work of some insidious and diabolical intelligence. It is titled, "As the Crow Stays.":

> A report of a revivalist meeting in a provincial newspaper ended as follows: "For upwards of an hour after the audience had dispersed, a large crow remained on the platform singing, "Abide With Me."

God knows that things have not been going well for the Evangelicals lately, and they certainly do not need even a syllable of gratuitous opprobrium; but facts are facts, even when they are mistakes, and if a large religious crow has been sighted and listened to, then people should know about it. We must learn to take inspiration where we find it. Or hear it. Or see it.

The other report that Sitwell plucked from the circumambient noise of printed verbiage is also worth passing on. I believe Mark Twain, especially, would have enjoyed it, for did he not write a booklet titled, *English as She is Taught*, taking his title from a Portuguese language phrase book? Sitwell's offering is titled, "Famous Sentences":

> Superb sentences are to be found in the dry pages of a Baedeker. What could be better than this from *Spain and Portugal?* "The traveller is warned against over-indulgence in fruit, alcohol, or other dietetic peccadillos." It is on a par with the English-Spanish conversation book which has this sentence, "Innkeeper, our postilion has been struck by lightning!"

I disagree with Mr. Sitwell's judgment. As good as the peccadillo sentence is, it is not on a par with the postilion sentence. *Nothing* is. That sentence is cast in golden moonshine and should never be disturbed.

The distance between Roy, the protagonist of *High Sierra*, and Sacheverell Sitwell is greater than that between Lake Erie and the Pacific Ocean. I speak of psychological/geographical distance, rather than size; because I am not clear about the relative magnitude of the two, nor of their cogent reality, though one is explicitly fictional and the other not. But, their relative realities notwithstanding, Keats seems to me as distant from Sacheverell Sitwell as he is from Roy. So an equilateral triangle might serve as a two-dimensional model of the relative qualities of these men, two of whom were actual and the other invented.

I believe that this connection of human and geographical features so distant from one another once again demonstrates that discrepancy is the essence of humor, as it is of much that is interesting in life. And I consider it an encouraging sign that so much discrepancy seems to be going around these days. It livens things up, just as it always has.

And the best part is, we don't ever seem to run out of discrepancies, especially in an election year. Discrepancies are a renewable resource, like timber and politicians. I think this is as cheerful a note as one could expect to end with, and I feel just a little bit privileged that I have found it to end with here. But to add to the good news, it is said that Lake Erie is much cleaner than it was a decade ago. As for the Pacific Ocean, however, it would be difficult to say. It's just too big; you can't see across it, even from 35,000 feet.

❦ St. John of the Appletrees

Various charity stores lie in wait for beginning book collectors who are tantalized by the certain fact of general public ignorance about rare books conjoined with the uncertain policy of such stores in stocking used books. In the past, such a conjunction often worked to the benefit of a collector with more time than money, or more hope than judgment. And, in spite of great spans of time wasted in driving to such stores (I speak of those under the auspices of Goodwill, Salvation Army, Volunteers of America, and the St. Vincent DePaul Society) and pawing over their sad accumulations of used books, I have nevertheless come upon a few buys that have momentarily seemed to justify such foraging. Two that immediately come to mind are *The History of the Hocking Valley*, Chicago, 1883, an important title for one interested in this region and its heritage, and Ludwig Bemelmans' *The Donkey Inside*, NY, 1941. The latter was Viking's special limited edition, with an original color illustration by Bemelman tipped in. This one cost me only five cents, which is to say, one nickel.

Although I haven't been able to break myself entirely of such excursions (hope here, as in life generally, keeps breaking through with vulgar insistence), I don't frequent these stores with anything like the regularity of my early booking years. Thus it is with something like nostalgia that I recall the last *old* rarity that I discovered in one of these likely/unlikely places. It happened about twenty years ago in a St. Vincent DePaul store in that generally run-down part of Columbus immediately west of the Scioto River that once bore the descriptive name of "The Bottoms." Perhaps it is still called that by old-timers.

As for the book itself, it remains in my possession. It has the unmistakeable character of old calf, the first glimpse of which had prompted me to pull it out from the shelf on that day long ago. . . and, of course, purchase it immediately. Its title was, and remains, "*The Doctrine of the New Jerusalem Concerning the Lord.* Translated from the Original Latin of the Hon. Emanuel Swedenborg, with Remarks Collected out of Other Works of the Same Author, By the *Rev. William Hill.*" And, as stated at the bottom of the title page, it was printed "For a Member of the New Jerusalem Church" in Philadelphia in 1815.

So far, you have read nothing that might explain a twenty-year-long memory, even if this was the last, or latest, pre-1850 book I've purchased for a quarter in a charity store. Most of the religious books from this period are wonderfully unreadable. And an 1815 Philadelphia publication date is practically yesterday.

However, on the verso opposite the title page, in old ink so faded by age that it is almost as light as foxing, is written: "Nathaniel Chapman, His Book." On the fly leaf at the end is written, "C. Cincinnati," with the ornate capital "C" repeated several times beneath, suggesting a sort of holographic stuttering.

Given the text, the name, and the date, it is almost certain that this book was once the property of the half brother of John Chapman, better known as the legendary "Johnny Appleseed." Nathaniel Chapman was in some ways more than a sibling, however; he was a close companion who had immigrated with Johnny Appleseed westward over the mountains, and then accompanied him on many of his travels throughout Ohio in the early 1800's.

Nathaniel eventually settled at Duck Creek in Washington County, north of Marietta (founded by cultivated New Englanders and named for Marie Antoinette), during the early years of the century. Although Johnny continued wandering all his life, tax records and other documents show that Nathaniel settled down on Duck Creek, along with their father, also named "Nathaniel."[1]

Johnny Appleseed and his half-brother Nathaniel were both members of the Church of the New Jerusalem; that is, they were "Swedenborgians." Although it is hard to distinguish fact from folklore in the many stories about Johnny Appleseed, it is obvious that he marched, not only to a

1. My copy could not have belonged to the father, for he died in 1807. See Robert Price's, *Johnny Appleseed: Man and Myth*, Bloomington (In), 1954, p. 62.

different, but to a Heavenly drummer. He was, in fact, something of a cranky mystic, a holy man obsessed with apples, a peculiar sort of protestant frontier saint, indifferent to the hardships of penury or the amused contempt of others as he wandered all over the midwest planting apple trees in all directions. For this habitude he eventually became so famous that it provided the inspiration for his nick-name. What is less known, however, is the fact that he also sowed the seeds of many medicinal herbs, including "unfortunately, the noxious weed dog-fennel."[1]

Henry Howe in his *Historical Collections of Ohio* (first published in Cincinnati in 1847, the year Johnny Appleseed died) wrote about this extraordinary man; and Howe's historical credibility is respectable, for he himself rode on horseback throughout the state, gathering data about local history as he went. His description is further corroborated in that it agrees with everything that is elsewhere written about Johnny Appleseed:

His personal appearance was as singular as his character. He was a small "chunked" man, quick and restless in his motions and conversation; his beard and hair were long and dark, and his eye black and sparkling. He lived the roughest life, and often slept in the woods. His clothing was mostly old, being generally given to him in exchange for apple trees. He went bare-footed, and often travelled miles through the snow in that way. In doctrine he was a follower of Swedenborg, leading a moral, blameless life, likening himself to the early Christians, literally taking no thought for the morrow. Wherever he went he circulated Swedenborgian works, and if short of them, would tear a book in two and give each part to different persons. He was careful not to injure any animal, and thought hunting morally wrong. He was welcome every where among the settlers, and treated with great kindness even by the Indians.[2]

Not only was Johnny Appleseed a vegetarian, as one might infer from his views on hunting, but—according to an anecdote Howes relates—he was so scrupulous against taking life that upon one occasion he doused

1. *Dictionary of American Biography*. Vol. 4, pp. 17, 18.
2. p. 432.

his fire in the woods when he saw mosquitos flying into it and burning to death.

One of the strangest gestures in Howes' account is Johnny Appleseed's tearing of Swedenborgian texts apart for distribution, suggestive of the distribution of shoots and cuttings from apple trees so that they might take root or be grafted upon old stock and thrive for the spiritual nourishment of generations to come. The thought of tearing a book apart is generally a nasty one; however, given the realities and general intellectual impoverishment of frontier life, it is not unpleasant to think that the dissemination of these two sorts of text—one physical and botanic, the other textual and spiritual—came out of the same benign impulse for sharing and disseminating the truth as one knows it.

These two sorts of gesture also reflect one of the central tenets of Swedenborg's philosophy, that all physical objects in our world are symbols of spiritual realities. Although Swedenborg claimed divine revelation (it is said that sometimes he would remain day and night in a sort of coma), there is an obvious analogy to Platonist and Neo-Platonist cosmology in this view of the symbolic character of the physical world.

Swedenborg's philosophy has fascinated many who are more famous than he. In one way or other, he influenced William Blake, Coleridge, Balzac, Henry James Sr., and—perhaps most of all—Emerson. Independent of his visions and their religious import, Swedenborg's theories seem to evoke response from people of both analytical and imaginative temperaments, especially when these temperaments are conjoined in the same mentality.

❧   This Swedenborgian connection is interesting to me personally as well as bibliophilically. While I am not a member of the Church of the New Jerusalem, nor am I intimately familiar with its doctrines, I did teach for five years at a Swedenborgian institution years ago. This was Urbana College, in Urbana, Ohio. While there, I met and became close friends with Bjørn Johannsen, a Swedenborgian minister who often joined me in my booking excursions. He was in his seventies, and I was approximately half his age. But the difference in ages was unimportant, for he was a man of rare qualities and a rare companion on these booking forays.

Once, when we stopped for lunch in a small coffee shop near Findlay, Ohio, the waitress asked if we wanted apple pie for dessert, and the Rev. Johannsen answered—in a heavy bass voice and with an extraordinarily plosive Icelandic accent—"Only if it was made from apples that came from trees that Johnny Appleseed planted." As I remember it, the waitress didn't seem to be sure what he was talking about. But then, the problem might have been more his accent than her ignorance.

Bjørn Johannsen was a fine man, wise and principled beyond the reach of most. He was magnanimous, tolerant, and possessed of a genial humor. Shortly before he died, he preached his last sermon to his Swedenborgian congregation in Cincinnati, and it is reported that only a small scattering of perhaps half a dozen parishioners were there to hear him. This fact seems to me very sad; but then I suspect that Bjørn would have been able to handle it better than most. I would like to believe that some values are beyond the reach of numbers and popularity—that general acceptance, or the lack thereof, is as irrelevant to their validity as the latest women's fashions from Paris are to the earth's gravitational field.

A few years after Bjørn Johannsen died, I dedicated one of my novels to his memory.

🍎   Johnny Appleseed has fired the imagination of many writers, especially those from the midwest, who can still feel (or *feel* they can feel) his influence in their native region. He was in truth an uncommon man by almost any measure. Few people have lived so selfless and dedicated a life, and have sustained their principles so fervently. Is it any wonder that poems and plays have been written about him, or that he has walked in and out of countless histories and novels?

Certainly, he fits more comfortably into a work of fiction than into histories, for most that is remembered about him is extravagant, melodramatic, sentimental, and, at its worst extreme, cute and sappy. I am aware of the temptation to borrow his existence for fiction, for I once cast him for a cameo role in one of my short stories, titled "Lucinda Hill Is Born

Again,"[1] in which he is come upon sitting "all alone in a rocking chair by a creek, eating a dish of mashed potatoes and gravy."

He is a wonderful character to use in certain ways, for he is almost more symbol than fact; and he can be turned this way and that, like a diamond, to show different facets of what he was, or might have been. It is hard not to make use of him, if you write a certain kind of story that takes place in the Ohio Valley in the early nineteenth century.

But of course you don't have to write fiction to make use of him. He is a wildly poetic figure, at odds with the world, and yet containing himself as few people ever have. Vachel Lindsay knew this, and so have many others. Thus it is perhaps only natural that I have made use of him in other ways. For example, I was once inspired to write a poem about him, in which I tried to convey something of his awful restlessness of spirit (somewhat analogous to that of the early circuit riders in their response to the call to go forth and preach), the cold wholesome purity of his obsession with apples, and his single-minded pursuit of a dream that strikes most people as odd, foolish, and trivial. I tried to suggest that in some ways Johnny Appleseed was as distant from the rest of us as we are from animals. My poem ends naturally with his death, followed by lines which state that when his body rotted, the smell of apples reached all the way from Pennsylvania to Wisconsin.

But I have a special feeling for another verse that jingles and is dangerously close to doggerel. It is possessed of its own homegrown eloquence and therefore deserves to be quoted in its entirety. This is the memorial inscription of the Johnny Appleseed Memorial Commission of the Washington County Pioneer Association, dedicated on September 27, 1942. After all that gargling, the inscription itself is wonderfully brief, clear, and to the point:

> Without a hope of recompense
> Without a thought of pride
> John Chapman planted appletrees,
> And preached, and lived, and died.

It seems appropriate to end a brief celebration of Johnny Appleseed by way of poetry, but there is one further comment I would like to make.

1. In *Tales of the Ohio Land*, Ohio Historical Soc., Cols., 1980.

Obviously, my preoccupation with this strange and mysterious figure has not been contained by the references I have made in the past, for there is this present occasion, in which I have referred to those other writings, and have even quoted from them.

So now I have personally written about Johnny Appleseed three times; and yet, these three times have not been sufficient. Much more remains to be said, and—beyond that—far more to be contemplated. It is this felt plenitude that has made him worth writing about in the first place; and it is this same plenitude that has shown how he is too odd and distant from us for a clear image to emerge, no matter how many times we strive to embody what he was, whether in prose or verse.

But while the fragments are obviously, in one sense, not enough, and merely tantalize us with what they suggest, they are, in another way, not only sufficient, but exactly right. The sense of the paradox is this: there are some things—some values and some people—that are best seen only partially.

I refer to those great congregations who are absent when a wise and gentle old Swedenborgian minister preaches his last sermon. And this truth also applies to fragments of information caught like burrs in the texts of a hundred books, extending even to that most peripheral of clues, the signature in an old book on Swedenborgian doctrine of a man who was probably, though not certainly, John Chapman's half-brother.

These hints are precisely enough for certain kinds of lore. Here is a truth that Swedenborg himself embraced, for he argued that the great panorama of the physical world was only representational, thereby suggestive of another, vaster and more marvelous one. Thus, insofar as we are rational creatures with a capacity for wisdom, it is our business to contemplate this Absence with all our minds.

🐦 Perhaps the Greatest
Incomparable Autobiography
in the World

After a recent foray into darkest Ohio's Licking and Muskingum Counties, in search of old and rare books, I recorded the event and mileage in my notebook, and then graded the day's success as "C–." This grade represents my judgment of the value and interest of the books procured relative to the mileage and time expended in the search. Possibly my best book was a first edition in dust jacket of James Gould Cozzens' *The S. S. San Pedro*, New York (1931). The binding is faded at the edges, but the dj is near mint.

This book is far from being a spectacular rarity (Van Allen Bradley does not even list it in the third edition of his *Handbook of Values*—although he lists other Cozzens titles); still, after coming upon it in this way, I read it and found it a readable if rather peculiarly truncated novel from that time. It belongs to the class of "sea novels" that provided some of my favorite reading when I was young. This class includes such obvious masterpieces as *Moby Dick, The Nigger of the Narcissus,* and *The Sea Wolf* (which I read from an old Armed Forces edition while a radioman on a Coast Guard cutter on anti-submarine patrol in the North Pacific—the very scene of the novel's action—during World War II), along with such lesser-known books as Marcus Goodrich's *Delilah*, Nicholas Monsarrat's *The Cruel Sea*, and Conrad Aiken's fine, famously neglected novel, *Blue Voyage*.

It is worth something to have a copy of Cozzens' book with the dj in such fine condition. Dust jackets from even so late a period are possessed of a certain rarity and aesthetic charm. I paid a Zanesville dealer only $4 for this book—something of a bargain; and yet, if it is judged the best of some forty titles I bought that day, and if one considers the further "expenditure" of 170 miles and some six hours' driving and digging through piles of old books, the grade of C– seems generous enough. I have had students who have been well content with receiving a C–.

But like all grades, that C– is fundamentally mysterious. Since it is my own private code, I understand at this moment pretty clearly what it means. It is now clear enough, although I am aware that within months I will not be able to recall any of the other titles I bought that day; and with the passage of years, even *The S. S. San Pedro* will likely founder and sink into oblivion, for I don't think I'll decide to keep the book in my private collection and seriously undertake collecting the first editions of James Gould Cozzens. There are knowing people who do collect him, but I don't believe I'll ever be among them.

No one can easily predict the memory's future, however. Out of every ten "good" novels (the class to which I have assigned *The S. S. San Pedro*) you read, will there be one that you will think about occasionally, without being cued in some way? Will there be a scene or idea or character that will recur to you at odd moments, having become part of . . . not just your mental furniture, but the inventory of your awareness? And if some part of a novel does surface in your mind, now and then, carrying associations of the entire text, in the way of synecdoche, is this alone indicative of your true and abiding esteem for the book? Or is the issue clouded by other mysterious factors at work in the memory, so that it is possible that a novel not even thought of for years might bob to the mind's surface and announce its re-emergence with a silent shock of pleasure—causing you to wonder how you could have not thought of it for so long, when others have been riding along with you, more or less permanently visible and unforgotten?

There are no precise answers to such questions, as we all know; but that does not prevent their insisting upon being asked. These are murky matters, and far from the clearest issue implicit in them is that of one's grading system. How, understanding the problematic, uncertain, and time-troubled character of events, could I, for example, have the gall to *grade* them? Is this simply a habit I have acquired from years of teaching, during which time I have learned to be comfortable with such labels? If you do anything long enough, it begins to seem natural. According to a *graffito* I encountered years ago, "God grades on a curve." Let's hope so. And if we are made in his image, it's no wonder that we go around instinctively, unconsciously grading everything in sight—and some things out of sight—

including new model sports cars, sunsets, a momentary mood, news reports on television, submarine sandwiches, a committee meeting, and the
day's weather. Is this possible?

Well, the answer is yes, sort of. We simply go around grading everything.
"Judge not that ye be not judged," sure . . . but it is evidently humanly
impossible not to grade the things about us (including Super Bowls,
bicycles, and mothers) in some way, at some level. Not all people may be
as literally grade-stricken as we teachers are; but there is evidence that all
people instinctively *sort* of sort out and judge the things about them,
whether they are moments or things or events, and whether they themselves are aware of doing so or not, and quite independently of their
intending to package all of their wildly differents sorts of experience in
such crude but tidy ways.

Since there's no avoiding it, the only sensible pragmatic conclusion is that
there is nothing essentially wrong with such grading—providing, that is, we
never quite lose sight of the fact that it is a sort of game we're playing. To
lose sight of this fact eventuates in all kinds of unfortunate confusions. And,
even though I am certain that all sensible people must be aware of this, it
seems to me that the overwhelming evidence points to the fact that all of us
consistently, even relentlessly, fail to pay attention to it. We talk as if it were
not a fact at all. We go around making statements that are utterly incompatible with this simple truism, no matter how clearly we understand that such
statements simply cannot mean what they are presumed to mean.

What I am referring to is the heresy, the essential stupidity, of constant,
unreflective quantification, which is best exemplified by the ever popular
Guinness Book of World Records. (It is also manifest in the currently popular
superstition of "the bottom line"—a perfectly useful and valid conclusive-
ness in some contexts, but woefully simple-minded in others.) The fact
that I grade booking expeditions proves that I have no right to refer
condescendingly to this lust to quantify, as if I am above such things. To
be above such things is to be out of touch with the majority, and to be
entirely out of touch with the majority, is to be judged (which is to say, is
to *be*) insane. In this context, judgment of others (a *consensus gentium*) is
everything. The ancient Greeks understood this, which is implicit in their
word *idiotes*—meaning "private" to the extent of being "peculiar"—a
meaning refracted vestigially in our words "idiom" and "idiot."

No, we are all fascinated by and committed to the cult of quantification. I understand it and acknowledge its importance in collecting first editions. First appearances, like first impressions, have a special authority. We are fascinated with priorities, and acknowledge their special power in virtually every conceivable context. Who would not cherish owning a copy of the first known document published in Louisiana—a 1768 broadside in both English and French, declaring amnesty for English army deserters? Who would not covet a copy of the first play published in Missouri? (*The Pedlar: A Farce in Three Acts*, by Alphonso Wetmore was published in St. Louis in 1821 and features a "rastlin" match between a boatman and a constable named "Opossum.")

First things possess a natural luster for us. Learning that the first paleontology report was prepared by Cotton Mather, describing three teeth and a 17-foot thigh bone found in Albany, New York (he thought they were remains from a race of giants), we are unmoved by similar reports published a year or two later.[1]

I am as enchanted by the extremes of human endeavor as others presumably are, and when I read in the *Guinness Book of World Records* that "the longest sentence ever to have gotten past the editor of a major newspaper is one of 1,286 words in *The New York Times*, by Herbert Stein in the issue of Feb. 13, 1981," I am contemptuous of any sentence of lesser length.[2] More than mere sensationalism is at work here; there is a natural human interest in exploring the extremes of the human condition. I feel somehow edified when I learn that Morris Katz, the world's most prolific portrait painter, had sold, as of March 5, 1984, 131,652 portraits. Learning this, I am instructed in one dimension of human accomplishment, even though few of us approach Mr. Katz in industry . . . and even though it might well be true that not one of those portraits would impress me as being worth doing. Still, they must have favorably impressed enough people to populate a city, for these portraits are said to have been sold, which means there must have been folks who bought them. But above and

1. See Joseph Nathan Kane's *Famous First Facts*, 4th Edition, Expanded and Revised, New York, 1981.
2. Although Faulkner has a longer one in "The Bear" and Joyce has written "sentences" far longer than that.

beyond their financial worth, they have been *done*—and considering their simple, dumb, enormous quantity, that is something.

Nevertheless, even as we respond to such linear attainments, and take pleasure in what they represent, or at least suggest, we should not give our minds wholly to them. They function successfully only when it is understood that they are part of a game being played, and we should never forget the tacit rules of the game. The need to measure is a very great and powerful one, and it is possessed of its own functional importance, and even—at times—beauty.

And yet, such measurements are devoid of nuance and subtlety. Katz's hundred thousand portraits do not make him a great painter, only a prolific one. And no one could doubt that it would be folly to suppose that a 200,000 word novel is necessarily twice as good as one of half that length. Nevertheless, sheer size is often a factor in describing a particular work as "minor" or "major"; and we just as uncritically judge and classify books according to some tacit scale of hierarchy. We do so casually, thoughtlessly, instinctively, just as if we were counting quarters or weighing melons.

Consider the familiarity of such statements as "Joyce is the greatest master of prose in the 20th century"; or, "Shakespeare is the greatest literary genius who ever lived." Many thoughtful people would agree with the first assertion, and still more would agree with the second. But how seriously can such assertions be viewed? Not very. Since literature is itself a game with tacit though flexible and changing rules (thus the opportunities for innovation by writers and constant re-evaluation by readers and critics), it would be hard to arrive at a clear understanding of what criteria should be used and how they should be applied to various works created in various situations with various intent.

Possibly the greatest benefit to the clarity and honesty of our judgments would be the deletion of the word "greatest" from our vocabulary. But how much all of us would miss it! The word serves a deep emotional need expressive of either some momentary enthusiasm or a conventional judgment that is itself better left unjudged. Furthermore, it tidies up our value systems, which are constantly threatened by a bewildering, naughty, and ragged world; and it helps us believe for an instant that we are more coherent and better integrated in our values than we really are. Intimately related to the myth of "bottom line" thinking, the word "greatest" gives us a brief, blissful mind massage, creating an impression that we are realistic and even hard-headed. And there is nothing like a mind massage for a hard head.

I am afraid that the cult of linearity is something we have to learn to live with. Even the most sensible people will, upon occasion, fumble their wits and blither away as if they didn't know a linear premise from New England style clam chowder. The estimable Wright Howes, whose *US-iana* is a model of scholarship wedded to mercantile judgment, is guilty. In his entry for John Woolman's *Works*, he terms the old Quaker's famous *Journal* (included therein): "An autobiographical masterpiece, rivalled in eighteenth century America only by that of Franklin."

The term "rivalled only" betrays this good man. If one is to take it literally (and how else *is* one to take it, since the words are there?), then one must assume that Howes has read all eighteenth century American autobiographies—a stultifying notion! Furthermore, we are presumably meant to assume that he has read them with unvarying attentiveness and sympathy, and out of the same fund of knowledge and insight, relative to the authors . . . has read them all and arrived at this final and reasoned judgment! "Rivalled only" means that Woolman's and Franklin's autobiographies are the two greatest of the eighteenth century, and all others are categorically, demonstrably, and measurably less. But had Howes read John Churchman's *Account and Gospel Labours* when he expressed himself so pontifically? (It is not listed in his book, and I doubt that he had.) Or did he read it two days after returning the proof-read galleys of *US-iana*, then suffer an apocalyptic seizure, snap his fingers, and cry out to his wife something like: "Damn! This is a better one than Woolman's, but it still isn't any better than Franklin's!"

I would like to think something like this happened, because I am convinced that Churchman's book (published in Philadephia, 1779) is, indeed, a better book, by almost any standard, than Woolman's. However, it is not nearly so famous as Woolman's—which is a book that has been praised by such impressive witnesses as Charles Lamb and Alfred North Whitehead. But so what? Had *they* read Churchman's book? Probably not, but we'll never know.

What can you believe in if you can't believe in the syllabi of college level English departments and their canonized writers and institutionalized classics? Well, you can become a sophisticated reader and then learn to believe in your own witnessing. Quakers, especially, will understand this. Or would have, at one time. Also, Methodists and other dissenters who believed in "doing their own thing" long before that disgusting cant phrase became the battle cry of a generation of benighted and unruly children.

But even in those early days, a heroic ignorance was not without danger. If enough people praised a specific book, one had better know something about it or forfeit his or her intellectual self-respect. Acknowledged "classics" constitute a literary sort of truism, and truisms are not necessarily false simply because they are obvious and therefore evoke the babbling distrust of intellectuals. Almost a century after Woolman's and Churchman's autobiographies were published, Schopenhauer wrote, "If a man smiles a lot, he's happy." Sigmund Freud, two generations after *that*, would not have been able to cope with this utterance (for reasons that are both interesting and not totally devoid of worth) . . . but, independently of these aphorisms, we have an abiding intellectual obligation to pay attention to common sense, even as we understand how limited and, upon occasion, perfidious it can prove to be.

❦   Part of the problem with linear measurements, crudely encoded in the comparison of adjectives (great, greater, greatest) has to do with the radical diversity of works of art. Even those which are comparable in important ways (e.g., Woolman's and Churchman's) will succeed precisely as they convey and render vivid the unique characters and fates of their subjects. Therefore, the more successful they are, the more individual they are, which is to say, the less basis they provide for comparison. Isn't this precisely what we ask of a good book? And isn't this especially important in biography or autobiography—that we ask for those unique and telling characteristics that have made our subject important and interesting? The converse of this is true as well: as in all our reading, we crave a sense of the common, shared humanity of the subjects, because this is necessary for our understanding them, as well as for our assimilating what they thought and felt about the human condition, and how they tried to cope with the difficulties we are all in some way faced with, and how they set about to solve the eternal human problems that are to some extent, and in some way, manifest in all our lives. (If they were not, they could not be referred to as "eternal"—of course; but circular arguments are often useful, as I hope this is.)

Biographies and autobiographies can have as many sorts of excellence as humans themselves. This is a fact so obvious that it needs constant repetition. (See the remarks on truisms and circular argumentation, above.) I have read wonderful books in the twofold *genre* (of bio/ autobiographies) that are virtually unknown. A sample listing would include, *Mason Long, Converted Gambler* (Chicago, 1878—this is also good Civil War material); *The Last of the Old West,* by George Mecklenburg (Wash., 1927—"The West has been fenced and plowed and ruined for adventure," the dust jacket states); and *The Autobiography of a Little Man* (he wasn't), by R.R. Wyatt, M.D. (np, nd).

And then there's *Marse Henry,* by Henry Watterson (2 vols, New York, 1919). I came upon this book somewhere in the slush and picked it up, inferring from the title that it was southern Americana, and would be a nice item for trading on one of our visits with our eldest daughter and her family in Snellville, Georgia. However, I picked it up and started to read it, and from the vantage point of trading, that was a mistake. "In a class by itself," we say of such a work; or we call it "incomparable," and then promptly forget what these phrases mean and proceed to classify and compare it.

But Watterson's book is so obviously unique that even the most taxonomophilic of us are reluctant to categorize it. Although it is explicitly autobiographical, I had to go to the *Dictionary of American Biography*—after I had finished reading it—in order to find out something about the man's life. It is truly a most curious book, but utterly, irresistibly fascinating from beginning to end. As an account, it is superbly flawed—chaotic, anecdotal, rambling, and gossipy. It is so blown by the winds of impression that without Watterson's occasional insertion of dates, a reader would have absolutely no idea where in the course of his career an event takes place.

It is in truth a literary oddity, a sport without issue. Essential information is lacking all over the place. A reader has almost finished the book before discovering that Watterson was married and had a family. Then it is revealed that the old scoundrel had been married 54 years, as of the writing, having been married in Chattanooga in the winter of 1863–4, while "The War of Sections" (as Watterson insisted it should be termed) was raging at its most intense.

If his wife had a first name, I don't remember its ever being mentioned. However, the reader is told that ,"She had a fine contralto voice and led the church choir." There is also reference to "conjugal felicity"; but, while there are photos of Watterson himself, along with a good view of his library at "Mansfield" (in Kentucky) and the likeness of a man whom I can't remember being mentioned in the text (it's as if he's wandered in from some other account), there are no photographs of the family.

It isn't only his wife who is neglected. Halfway through the second volume, there is this casual reference: "I had not then lost the action of one of my hands." One of his hands? There's no reference before this to such a crippling injury or illness, nor is there further clarification. Maybe he injured it in action near Chattanooga. Watterson had been a soldier on the Confederate side, where he'd fought hard for a while, but had then (undergoing interesting if somewhat disoriented adventures) come over to the Union side. I think that was when he was headed for England for some reason, although I'm not sure.

I am sure that he was a brave and good man, however. His loyalty to Dixie had nothing to do with a taste for slavery, which he despised; and it was somewhat aloof from his conviction that there was no possible way for the South to win. The problem was politics—which Watterson knew and understood well enough to despise with articulate and whole-hearted conviction. "I have declaimed not a little in my time," he wrote, "about the ignoble trade of politics, the collective dishonesty of parties, and the vulgarities of the self-exploiting professional office hunters."

This is clear enough, and disgruntled enough. But then, Watterson was practically raised in Washington, and had the gift of getting to know everybody and understanding more of the human spectrum than is common. He was also something of a personal rebel with far greater conviction than he could manage as a Rebel. With an odd, Whitmanesque flourish, he states, "I suppose I must have been born an insurrecto."

Watterson's genius for anecdote and his appetite for humanity were prodigious. The first chapter heading states: "I am Born and Begin to Take Notice." And by God he was and did! (I think it was this that got me started, and the promise in that heading was never broken.) He knew something about everyone and knew how to tell about it. As an old man, he bore a striking physical resemblance to his kinsman and contemporary, Mark Twain—whom he knew, of course. His aunt had married Twain's uncle, so he spoke with authority when he wrote of Twain's mother that she "was the loveliest old aristocrat with a taking drawl, a drawl that was high-bred and patrician, not rustic and plebeian, which her famous son inherited. All the women of that ilk were gentlewomen. The literary and artistic instinct which attained its fruition in him had percolated through the veins of a long line of silent singers, of poets and painters, unborn to the world of expression until he arrived upon the scene."

Well, there was nothing silent about *this* singer, nor did Watterson ever hesitate to pronounce authoritatively upon the events of his time. Again speaking of Twain, he called him "a medley of contradictions," and then somehow managed to compare him to Abraham Lincoln. Well, it takes one to know one.

As a youth, Watterson states, he had ambitions to be a novelist. He loved the art of fiction, and throughout his life remained, in his own words, "a voracious novel reader." But as for his own career as a novelist, he claims that he failed. And, while it is true that he never "became" a novelist in the manner of his famous cousin, the reader of his autobiography may be inclined to disagree with his assumption that he really failed—not because the old man tells lies or has in some other way written a good novel in the present instance, but because he makes stories out of the past, and does so with the gusto and flair of the born tale teller.

Not only did he know everyone, but he knew how to tell about what he knew. He had an eye for detail and an ear for speech, and somewhere behind them all, he had a mind for tale spinning. Speaking of the famous actor, Joe Jefferson, Watterson writes: "His purpose was to fill the scene and forget himself." Such is the merit in Watterson's book . . . almost to a fault, you sometimes think, when you find yourself wandering from one delightful story to another, knowing that they've been spilled out upon the page with utter contempt for chronology and the conventions of good sound biography.

Whom did he know? Who not! He was with Artemus Ward during his last days in England, when the famous humorist was literally killing himself to be funny on the lecture circuit (much as Dickens did). Watterson's account of Ward's last days is eloquent and touching. And his insider's knowledge of American political life is the stuff and spirit of gossip. "No man of his time could hold a candle to Mr. Blaine in what we call magnetism . . . " he states magnanimously. But he hated Woodrow Wilson just as heartily as he approved of Blaine. He lines his memories up, as do most of us, in two files, featuring the good guys on one side and the bad guys on the other. Certainly there were enough scoundrels, fools, and villains for his wrath, and somewhere he reports on seeing everyone in the House (of Representatives) drunk. He also knew who the real "man who broke the bank at Monte Carlo" was—and most people merely thought he was a character in the popular song of that day. Of President Andrew Johnson, he wrote, "I knew him from childhood. Thrice that I can recall I saw him weep; never did I see him laugh." And later: "I do not believe a more conscientious man ever lived."

Watterson loved superlatives the way a painter might love primary colors, and he would not have entirely agreed with my thesis that underlies this paper. With breezy confidence, he deals out superlatives and rates the world with the eye of one who has been around and knows. He labels everyone as strikingly as his mood or memory nudge him. A pretty girl is not allowed to remain merely pretty, but is said to be "the prettiest girl in Washington"; the men he knew were the most brilliant or the most gifted or the most wretched . . . the most *anything*, in fact, that might liven the story or suit the context.

Outspoken, garrulous, opinionated, Watterson simmered with ideas and impressions. He rails against the corruption he has witnessed in high places, but never totally despairs. Despair might have stultified him, rendering him mute; and what would a natural-born story teller do then? Newfangled ideas irritated him mightily, and his reactions are those of any testy old man with convictions. Pious and patriotic, he reflects upon the Founders of the Republic, and writes contemptuously of those who "would displace the example of the simple lives they led and the homely truths they told, to set up a school of philosophy which had made Athens stare and Rome howl, and, I dare say, is causing the Old Continentals to turn over in their graves."

As this passage shows, Watterson was no more afraid of cliches than of inciting argumentation. He seemed, in fact, contemptuous of any fussy need to pay too close attention to diction and other small matters of style. One page of a letter he wrote to President Grover Cleveland contains enough tangled metaphors to trip up and scatter an entire cavalry regiment, but Watterson sails through with flags flying. "There is more than a fighting chance," he wrote encouragingly to the President. Then, a line or two later, he continued: "I can see daylight, if you will relax your grip somewhat upon the East and throw yourself confidently upon the West."

As his metaphors are mixed with one another, his cynicism is wonderfully mixed with hope. "Let us agree at once that all government is more or less a failure," he sturdily recommends; and he scorns those "preaching 'the prissy gospel of sweetness and light.' " Elsewhere, he sounds a modern note: "In a nation of undiscriminating voters the noise of the agitator is apt to drown the voice of the statesman. We have been teaching everybody to read, nobody to think." (Today, we would amend that last part to "nobody to read well"—but the meaning is essentially the same.) And yet, near the end of both his life and book, this same man writes: "The love of the ideal has not in my old age quite deserted me."

But we keep returning to what he remembers, the stories he has to tell: he tells of seeing John Wilkes Booth as a chronic, staggering drunk in the days before he killed Lincoln, and he gives his view of Tilden, claiming that he was too colorless ("there was nothing spectacular about Tilden") and too much of a philosopher king to be elected President. Then there is the story about Stephen Foster's "Scrapbook of Melodies," in which Watterson claims that the melody of one of Foster's most famous classics, "Old Folks at Home," was taken literally and without change from a posthumously published score by Schubert.

Watterson's instinct for a good story can skip a generation or two, as easily as any other part of his narrative; and he is naturally drawn to people with strong and colorful ways and vivid mannerisms—which is to say, those with whom he feels a spirited kinship. He quotes one of these, an old man known as Col. Walton, who'd been whipped by pirates years before. When asked what it was like, the old warrior replied: "Sir, they whipped me until I was perfectly disgusted."

The relentless flow of incident and reflection suggests a compulsive story teller—one who simply cannot resist a good yarn, especially if it is attached to one who is famous. But with Watterson, such is not exactly the case, for he possesses the yarn spinner's deeper and subtler ability to hint at things unsaid, if not unsayable. In short, he leads us to understand that he is possessed of secrets that are fascinating, but beyond telling. "I know of two Confederate Generals," he wrote, "who first tried for commissions in the Union Army; gallant and good fellows, too; but both are dead and their secret shall die with me." Such unheard melodies are sweet in prose as well as poesy, and it is a shrewd raconteur who can remind us of them.

Somewhere along the line, Watterson does mention his important connection with *The Louisville Courier Journal*—I believe he was instrumental in the merger from which it was formed and helped make it famous among newspapers. Furthermore, *The Dictionary of American Biography* gives clear evidence that he was far more than just a man-about-Washington with an extraordinary ear for gossip—he was an extraordinarily gifted newspaperman, as well. His influence during his life was great, although I would suspect he is largely forgotten today . . . except, perhaps, among historians of American journalism, and perhaps in Louisville.

But what an interesting man, and how worth knowing! Feminism was one of the great issues of his time, as it is now—on a quite different level, of course. How did Watterson feel about it? His endorsement of the cause was clear, yet cautious; for he feared "feminism" and disliked "professional females." He was perhaps too happy and well-adjusted a man to undertake revolutionary causes with the disgruntled passion they often seem to require. And yet his troubled advocacy of the franchise for women does not do him discredit, for he liked women very much precisely as they were and was afraid of their becoming imitation men. (This is, of course, a very dangerous argument; but then, most arguments are.)

Certainly, he loved controversy. He loved it naturally and full-bloodedly, beyond its usefulness to his instincts as a good journalist. On the eve of prohibition, speaking of the possibility of beer and wine pre-empting booze, the old curmudgeon wrote: "But gracious, this is getting upon things controversial, and if there is anything in this world that I do hybominate [*sic*], it is controversy."

Near the book's end, Watterson peeks out at the reader from behind his anecdotes, and evidently sees an expression of what might be simple consternation, or perhaps the beginning of something like disapproval. And suddenly it is revealed that he has known pretty much what he's been doing all along. "In bringing these desultory—perhaps too fragmentary—recollections to a close," he states, "the writer may not be denied his final word."

And who would have the heart to deny a final word to a man who was once "born and began to take notice"? Vividness and zest are what you get, and no sensible reader would trade this delightful adventure for any conceivable conventional, well-structured, literally informative account. After all, we can go to the *Dictionary of American Biography* for chronology and hard information; and after reading Watterson's book, we will certainly be forced to do just that . . . but when we do, we will go there cheerfully.

🍎 Cockfights, Hound Dogs, and Preachers

Only once in my life have I made a serious attempt to witness a cockfight. This was many years ago, and I knew very little about the sport, other than that it was both bloody and illegal—two facts that I understood might be connected. But I had heard that cockfights were held regularly in Athens and surrounding counties in southeastern Appalachian Ohio, and I thought it would be interesting to witness one and maybe even lose some money.

I don't usually think of myself as a criminal type, and I don't spend my days going around looking for laws to break; but in this, my curiosity was aroused: I wanted to witness a cockfight if I could arrange it. The issue, I realized, was somehow connected with my freedom. (All criminals think like this.) Moreover, as a writer I have a natural curiosity about such out-of-the-way things. We call it "gathering material."

Not only that, these fights were going to be held anyway, whether I saw them or not, and my presence would not add one teaspoonful to the bloodshed. The simple fact of my being among the spectators and bettors would not in itself cause the death of a single bird, would it? This is a dangerous argument, of course; but then, as I have argued two pages back, *most* arguments are dangerous. (This is, of course, in itself a dangerous argument. [Q.E.D.])

Since I don't have any known criminal connections (see paragraph above), I had to ask around, and eventually—as might have been predicted—I found out that there was a man who might be able to tell me where to go, and when. So I went to him, and he gave me the time of the next scheduled cockfight, along with highly detailed and probably accurate directions. He said I would know the last of many turns—this one onto a muddy township road to the right—by seeing where a sack of flour had been dumped in the road at the turn-off.

I wrote down the directions as given, and then this fellow and I talked about cockfighting awhile. He had gone to a number of fights, though not recently; and he'd enjoyed them. But then, he was a dedicated gambler and would enjoy just about any excuse for making a wager. He reminded me a little of Jim Smiley, in Mark Twain's famous account of "The Celebrated Jumping Frog of Calaveras County." I suspected that, like Jim Smiley, he'd bet on anything, "if he could get anybody to bet on the other side; and if he couldn't, he'd change sides."

What I'm saying is, this fellow was interesting and full of information, some of it possibly correct. He said that cockfights were held everywhere in Appalachia; he said that there was a mimeographed periodical that was mailed to people all the way from Ohio to Georgia and the Carolinas, and that cockfighting was well organized, even if it was illegal, and therefore somewhat secret. Evidently, there was a real underworld of cockfighting, somewhat like those more-famous, better advertised underworlds.

When he told me these things, it all seemed credible enough. There is visible evidence, in fact, and you don't have to drive on Township roads to see it. I am speaking of those barnyards where there are miniature villages of little wooden huts with fighting cocks chained to them. Some of these are within spitting distance of a state highway, if you can spit pretty far.

I thought of that other illegal Appalachian enterprise, moonshining, and asked myself, why shouldn't all of this be true? Wasn't I living within about thirty miles of New Straitsville, in Perry County, which advertises itself as the "Moonshine Capital of the World" and has an annual festival in celebration of this fact? Being the Moonshine Capital of the World is a curious thing to advertise or brag about, but I suppose people can take pride in almost anything, if they manage to look at it in the right way and find out how to exploit it. But the point was, for people in this area, cockfighting would be right down their alley. Even if places like New Straitsville don't have what you could really call "alleys."

At the scheduled time, I followed the directions I'd been given as well as I could. I drove and drove, and made a lot of turns onto hilly back roads. But for the life of me, I couldn't see any turn-off where a sack of flour had been dumped; so I finally gave up and came back home. I grumbled considerably to my wife, and mentioned that I knew somebody who was probably a hell of a lot better at gambling than he was at giving directions. She commiserated with me, although she was somewhat distant about it, as if she couldn't quite take such a disappointment seriously.

And the next day, she was sufficiently insensitive to call my attention to a small news item in the paper stating that on the previous evening seventy-five men had been arrested by the Sheriff at what was obviously the very cockfight I had been unable to find. "It's lucky you got lost," she pointed out, and I suppose she was right; although it's not the sort of thing a wife should make too much over.

🐓   Once, however, many years before this, I did witness a cockfight. This was entirely by accident; and I'll never forget it. It was early one summer morning in Urbana, Ohio, and I was standing outside a small supermarket at the edge of town, waiting for the store to open. Across the highway was an open field, and hearing a noise, I looked up and saw two cock pheasants running furiously opposite each other, clockwise on the circumference of an imaginary circle about thirty feet in diameter. Then, as if responding to some kind of signal, they rushed to the center, where they collided and furiously climbed each other ten or twelve feet straight up in the air; after which, they fell back and recommenced circling each other again. This was repeated several times, before they responded mutually to some other signal and fled the scene—the issue undecided, so far as I could tell. But they had not been equipped with razor-sharp steel spurs; and from what I've heard, if this had been a professional fight and they had been bred and trained fighters, one of them might well have been dead after that first closing when they'd climbed each other straight up, busily slashing as they rose.

I suspect that this is a scene which has been witnessed by few people in what might be termed "its natural state"; and I feel a modest, obscure sort of privilege in having witnessed it. Those cock pheasants were engaged in a ceremony that presumably has not changed at all during the millennia or two that cockfighting has been promoted as a blood sport. Those cock pheasants behaved totally outside of history (which is, after all, a human construct) . . . exactly as they would have behaved if Caesar had never lived or gunpowder had not been invented or thermonuclear weapons had not been devised. What I had witnessed was the primeval mating and territorial ritual that reflected the natural origin of the long and virtually universal history of cockfighting.

Appalachian culture inherited this bloody sport, like so much else, from England, where almost every town had its cockpit, where kings long enjoyed cockfighting as a royal entertainment. The term "battle royal," comes from the throwing of a dozen or so cocks into a pit and seeing which one survives—for it is the nature of these creatures that there cannot be two survivors. Also, the old expression of "showing the white feather"—denoting cowardice—is said to have come from the belief that birds with a single white feather (not birds with *all* white feathers) are timid.

Assuredly, it is a bloody sport, if it can be called a sport at all. But the posture of moral disapproval is so easy that it should be immediately suspect to any sensible person. If you breed a bird specifically for fighting, what else is he good for? And yet, the moral problem is already established: why breed them for fighting in the first place? Why not breed them sensibly for Chicken McNuggets or scrambled eggs fried with cheese, peppers, and onions?

But the moralists are the first to point out that the real damage is not the relatively swift killing of a somewhat brainless and useless bird, but the morally corrupting effect of witnessing this—and *enjoying it.*. In short, it is a brutalizing sport, and should be done away with. Most people today would agree with this; but there is a far older precedent that extends all the way back to the Puritans. Oliver Cromwell tried and nearly succeeded in abolishing it around 1650; but soon after his death and the re-establishment of the crown, it was taken up again by the gentry and mob alike, and became especially popular during the eighteenth century.

There were periods before its final prohibition by English law in 1849 when cocking was so popular that "mains" (as the matches were called) were held in churchyards on Sundays and at wakes and festivals, as well as in schools, some of whose pupils were given special allowances for buying their own fighting cocks.

Such a long and sustained tradition naturally inspired a vigorous literature. In his *Pleasures of Princes,* published in London in 1614, Gervase

Markham wrote, "Of the Choyce, Ordring, Breeding and Dyeting of the fighting-Cocke for Battell." In this quaint book (the first edition of which is very rare, and would probably fetch well over $1000, if one could be found), Markham writes with great expertise on how to make your bird a winner, displaying a sophistication not unlike that of current best sellers on how to make it big in the stock market. And why not? Where money is to be won, men are capable of great and clever attentiveness—or at least, the appearance thereof. After exercising your bird, Markham wrote, "Then let him sweate, for the nature of this scowring is to bring away his grease, and to breed breath, and strength." I consider this a wonderful passage, rendered even more remarkable by the fact that I have trouble in picturing just exactly how a fowl can manage to sweat.

Such birds have extraordinary pedigrees, and the bloodlines of many fighting cocks of the southern mountains can be traced back to England. This is especially impressive when one realizes that most cocks breed young and fight at one or two years of age. But old traditions are not necessarily venerable. Flogging, starvation, and various other tortures, along with imprisonment for debt and the hanging of petty thieves, have all been outlawed by the civilized world after centuries of custom, and few people would question that such abolishments are indicative of something in the way of human progress.

Should cockfighting be tolerated as a technically illegal but generally unenforced misdemeanor, or should it be seriously banned and go the way of flogging and imprisonment for debt? Clear thinking about such an issue is difficult, for it is troubled by the power and immediacy of images, which invite an easy sentimentality and often pre-empt clear thinking. No doubt there is a lot of bloodshed when one cock kills another, and I'm sure that the bloodlust of the crowd is far from attractive or edifying. On the other hand, those who are most eloquent in their disapproval strike me as being a canting, self-righteous, priggish lot; I am speaking of the Bambi lovers who would seem to be in serious danger of perishing from acute silliness, only their type lasts on and on through the generations, trying to instruct and edify those insensitive barbarians who have a similar durability.

You hardly know what to think. What I *don't* think is that I would have enjoyed being in Cromwell's company very long. But then, I don't think

I would have cared for Charles II, either. I must have very high standards for friendship. Or maybe neither of these men had the qualities necessary for true friendship, political power and royalty notwithstanding . . . or, quite possibly, *because* of political power and royalty. (I'm sure Cromwell and Charles II would have been disappointed to learn what I think about them.)

Nevertheless, it must be admitted that Cromwell's disapproval of pitting game cocks for sport was advanced for his time. Generally, humane treatment of animals is a modern concern, possibly related to the rise of secular humanism and a declining belief in the human soul. This connection is not unproblematical, for animal species were not the exclusive victims of man's viciousness and insensitivity. Instances of humane treatment of human beings—especially "the lower classes"—are seldom found before modern times.

I am here speaking not only of African slaves and the obviously downtrodden, but of a general brutality toward human kind, and an insensitivity that seems almost demonic to the modern western sensibility. In eighteenth century England, men, women, and children could be hanged for associating with gypsies or trespassing *with the intent* to kill rabbits. A seven year old of either sex could be sentenced to death for stealing a pocket handkerchief. And in 1777 a girl of fourteen was sentenced to be burned alive for hiding "whitewashed farthings" (presumably coins that had been meddled with to conceal defects or counterfeiting), but "was only reprieved by accident when the faggots were already laid."[1]

Throughout most of the history of England and America, indentured servants, apprentices, and the impoverished and helpless—a class which included virtually all children—have been mistreated generally, chronically, and pretty much as a matter of course. The mistreatment of children was, of course, excellent schooling for the perpetuation of cruelty to other children, when these grew up and they could pass on to a new generation what they themselves had been so brutally taught.

And yet, a literal belief in the human soul does theoretically set humankind apart from the rest of the animal world, thereby justifying a double

---

1. Pringle, Patrick. *Hue and Cry: The Story of Henry and John Fielding and Their Bow Street Runners.* Np (Bungay, Suffolk), nd., p. 11.

standard. Thus, with the denial of an immortal soul, humans become merely a more highly developed animal—a fact with two consequences: it makes us less noble in depriving us of a special relationship to God and Eternity, and it simultaneously raises the "lower animals" to a status of something like kinship, so that it is easier for us to sentimentalize over them.

Humanitarians are loathe to grade and evaluate the "quality of life" possessed by different creatures; this may be an extension of the democratic taboo against grading the quality of human lives. But most of us, nevertheless, would agree that it is a lesser wrong to kill a chicken than a human being. We grade different sorts of life whether we want to or not.

Albert Schweitzer, whose "reverence for life" was at the heart of his philosophy, was nevertheless a physician and medical missionary in Africa, and was obviously aware that in applying germicides in treating a human patient, he was destroying life at one level to preserve it at another.

Still, this is an ethical choice that can be defended (although it would be hard to convince a jury of germs), while breeding and raising cocks for the single purpose of fighting and killing others of their kind is a gratuitous act, and possibly a brutalizing one as well.[1] Maybe it's just as well I couldn't find that cockfight so many years ago; although—as with all unfulfilled impulses and sins of omission—I can't be sure of what price I've paid for not being there. Certainly, I missed paying the fine exacted from those seventy-five men who were caught; but there is also the possibility that if I had witnessed those cockfights before the Sheriff's arrival, I would have emerged from the experience a changed person . . . maybe I would have learned to hate cockfighting with the intensity of pious wrath we associate with Cromwell and his inflexible posture toward all that he viewed as sin and wickedness; maybe I would have even gotten to like Bambi . . . although that is almost too cruel to contemplate, and I would like to think that no matter what I had witnessed on that day, I would have proved too decent and strong to fall victim to so virulent a stupidity.

Maybe I would have become an *afficionado* of the pits ("pits" is another

---

1. This applies equally, of course, to the fighting of pit bulls—another old English pastime, but one—so far as I know—that has only recently gained popularity in the southern mountains.

term that derives from this ancient sport), a miscreant despised by all righteous citizens and pitied by those who are enlightened and understand what a wonderful thing it is to be a chicken and not subjected to such institutionalized indignities while being wagered upon by slavering rednecks.

❦   This brings us to the autobiographies of Appalachian preachers. Preachers, especially of the evangelical sort, have always tended to be obsessed with bearing witness; and it is not strange that many of them have undertaken to write their autobiographies upon retirement or in the ripe years of their ministry. Perhaps the burden of weekly sermons creates some mysterious pressure to write about oneself and one's past. Perhaps the garrulousness of authority leads naturally to some ultimate attempt to get it all down in words as clearly as possible—whatever "it" may be.

The autobiographical need is natural enough: we all want to talk about ourselves and convey to others something of our uniqueness and the essential mystery of what we are. This is only just and accurate, for the miracle is always there, even though for the reader of most attempts at autobiography, it verges upon being an act of faith to believe it.

In my booking experiences, I have come upon a great many autobiographies of preachers from the southern mountains. I have written elsewhere[1] about the itinerant preachers of the midwest who helped bring morality, literacy, and sobriety (although there are reports of early, pre-prohibition Methodist circuit riders who got so drunk they fell off their horses) . . . who helped bring civilization, that is to say, to the frontier beyond the mountains.

The folkways and habitudes of the early frontier midwest grew into sophistication and modernity by natural progression; but much of that same lifestyle has lasted on in the mountains, as vestigial as the Elizabethan idioms and old songs that were lost or fossilized in the rest of the English-speaking world. Thus, that curious *genre* of the Appalachian preacher's

1. *Booking in the Heartland*, Balt., 1986.

confessional autobiography, in which he recounts his own misadventures leading to salvation with the simplicity and purity of a morality play, has survived to the present day.

In part, this tradition extends back to Francis Asbury, who in 1784 made the first of his twenty journeys westward into the mountains and the land beyond. Asbury was a Methodist bishop, and a great man measured by almost any standard. On one of his later trips, in 1808, when he was sixty-three—a considerable age for that time—he came over the National Pike from Cumberland, headed west. His journal reads as follows:

> Thursday, June 30th: We breakfasted at four o'clock that we might climb the Allegany. Friday: Moved at four o'clock, after breakfasting. At five in the evening we landed at Jacob Murphy's our twenty-two hours ride had brought us seventy miles. I am pained and sore, and poor Jane stumbled so often. [He called all his horses "Jane."] On the Sabbath I preached at Uniontown. I spent the fourth of July at the Widow Henthorn's, reading and drafting Conference plans as far as Baltimore. On Tuesday I read Thomas A Kempis, and copied off a list of preachers for the western and southern conferences.[1]

Here is an extraordinary man, whose journal is worth quoting for several reasons, not the least of which is his habit of naming all of his horses "Jane." (How would this make a stallion feel? Or were they all mares?) But extraordinary men are by definition not true-to-type, and the type is what I am after at present. If it is a living text, the type will be both typical and unique, which is a healthy paradox for almost any sort of witnessing.

A better example for my purpose is a small, waterstained, paperback copy of a book I own, consisting of only 122 pages and titled *Sketches of My Life*, by George Peek, of Richwood, West Virginia. This small book was printed in Guthrie, Oklahoma—probably at the author's expense—and it does not bear a copyright date, although it is revealed in the text that it was likely printed in 1938 or 1939. The book is embellished by photographs, one showing George as a young hellion and the others showing him old, pious, and tame, surrounded by his considerable family.

1. Quoted in *Methodism on the Headwaters of the Ohio*, by Wallace Guy Smeltzer, Nashville, 1951. pp. 112, 113.

By now, we have come a long way from Bishop Asbury, both in time and sophistication. It is hardly conceivable that George Peek ever read Thomas A Kempis' *De Imitationi Christi*. Early in his account, he informs the reader of his own uncouth inadequacy as a writer, as follows: "My educational privileges were meager compared with those of today, as you no doubt will perceive before you get through with the gramatical blunders in this book." Although he spells "perceive" correctly, he does manage to misspell the word "grammatical"—giving it only one "m"—and thereby, simultaneously, giving a certain comfort to the reader, for it is evident that here is a writer with credibility . . . or "honesty," as we used to say.

George Peek is not a dull writer, although certainly not a gifted one. Nevertheless, he has his moments. I like the report he gives of his brief schooling, circa 1880, where he describes his fellow pupils, including the oldest boy, whose voice had changed:

> Joe had a man's voice; and as the custom was to spell and read aloud, we called him the "bumblebee." The other children had voices like honeybees when compared to his. I don't see how we learned anything. It would set me wild now. It sounded like a pond full of Pedeet frogs, with a great big bull frog sitting on the bank croaking with all its might.

I find this a wonderful scene, in its way—wonderfully apt in its description. Certainly, though; it is modest enough and can hardly be said to reach the heights of literary expression. Still, it is possessed of a sturdy and vivid directness that is refreshing.

Along with his uncouth ability as a writer, George Peek was a good worker, but he lacked specific skills as he lacked education, and spent most of his youth in hard labor, wanderlust, and dissipation. A later generation would have said he was searching for his identity, as if identity were a place like Elkins, West Virginia, or Chattanooga.

But as a sinner, George was only mediocre. For example, from the evidence given, he could never quite manage to be dishonest or malicious. Theft and homicide were beyond him. Insensitivity, he could attain to, along with a sort of down-home cussedness; but then he would ruin it all by feeling miserable and guilty immediately after doing something nasty. Nevertheless, as with most sinners, guilt and contrition did not always lead to reform. For example, his last reported backsliding was after he was married, when, to show off his emancipation from the evils of tobacco before a friend, George defiantly put a flake on his tongue. But the taste of the forbidden weed was too much for him. "It was not long," he wrote, "until I was drinking beer, playing cards, and shooting dice for money."

He was off the wagon for a year after this (which shows what a flake of tobacco can do), but then climbed back on and—according to the testimony, at least—led an exemplary life from then on, preaching the gospel and raising his family of seven children.

While still a bachelor, he had travelled a great deal, working three miles underground in a mine near Fairmont, West Virginia; working as a miner elsewhere for only 75 cents a day; wandering and finding work at hard (i.e., unskilled) labor at building bridges and railroads and working on a portable sawmill. He had some colorful times, and occasionally creates a scene of Hogarthian exuberance, as when he describes a drunken argument between a Mrs. Black and "an Englishman"—who is not further named—in Thomas, West Virginia. These two rowdies were on separate floors of a building and, according to Peek, got into an extended argument. They were so drunk that they couldn't move, but could only lie on their backs and yell insults at each other. George quotes Mrs. Black as crying out, "Dry up, you coyote, or I'll come up there and drag you downstairs!" to which the Englishman bellows, "Dry up down there, you bloody Irishman [sic], or I'll come down there and smather you like a boog." To which edifying dialogue, Peek adds the somewhat demure comment: "Neither one of them was able to get to the other if they had so desired."

Peek's autobiography is possessed of that symmetry that is essential to the *genre*, which is to say, it is as formulaic as an old-fashioned detective novel. The sinning has to be balanced by salvation, and the sinning must come first, so that it is remembered in a state of calm and wise acceptance . . . with the dark implication that, without so much wickedness, salvation would have no point. It is a familiar notion that the Devil is necessary for God to "exist against" in dialectic tension. Here we are in the familiar ontological room of transactional contraries: yes and no, off and on, being and nothingness, good and evil. The instant the Devil became a metaphor in the scienticization of liberal modern theology, the groundwork for the "death of God" was laid.

But here we are also in danger of drifting from our subject, for the Devil was quite real for George Peek. As real as God. The first harbinger of his calling was nearly drowning as a boy. It is unclear whether this drowning was the work of God or the Devil, for in the way of such things, it was morally ambiguous. But how it happened is interesting, and it is not hard to identify the Devil's instrument. One day, several boys went swimming together in a river. One of these boys, who knew that George couldn't swim, went out into the deep channel and treaded water, pretending he was standing on the bottom. He called out, assuring George it was shallow and urging him to wade on out to him. George complied, and the result would have been fatal if his cousin hadn't jumped into the river and saved him. So far as I know, the boy who'd tricked him isn't mentioned again in the book, but obviously he was an especially vicious and stupid type—perhaps mean enough to grow up and raise game cocks.

This experience for George Peek was a memorable one, of course. After being pulled from the river, he was thrown over a barrel to get the water out of his lungs. "Every mean thing I ever did came before me while I was struggling for life," he wrote. "I realized I was doomed for eternal night if I died then. I thought seriously about my condition for a while. However, I shook off the conviction and went on my way."

So the effects of this lesson were soon forgotten, and George launched upon his wandering and shiftless career as a ne'er-do-well. But the incident was not forgotten, and he would look back upon it as an initiation into those eschatological spectres of the Four Last Things: Death, Judgment, Heaven, and Hell. The final inspiration for his answering the call, however, was waiting for him some years in the future, when he came upon a street preacher in Clarksburg, West Virginia. George Peek does not say much about this man, but later, in referring to another preacher he admired, he expresses himself quaintly and memorably, saying, "He could picture a sermon as beautifully as most anyone I knew." That preaching can be viewed as an art should not be a surprise; but when a sermon is referred to as if it were visual instead of aural, a new way of looking at it is required, which is precisely what the genius of metaphor always requires of us.

George Peek seems to have been a good man, without the arrogance that is often implicit in a man who's convinced that he has a special calling. Peek is generous in his judgment of others and is possessed of a certain tact and dignified reserve that we can readily associate with the older folk of Appalachia. Though uneducated, he was not unintelligent; he studied the Bible earnestly, though obviously without the benefit of scholarship.

Such people as this often become cranks of the worst sort, for it is a general fund of knowledge and a general mastery of the skills of using information that prevent us from becoming "unbalanced"—which is to say, limited to a single perspective, unaware of the authenticity of others. This sort of thing can happen to ostensibly educated people as well as to quasi-literate Appalachian preachers, and you can attend an academic conference of chemists, anthropologists, economists, or literary critics and find little communication happening, except in certain narrow, intricately designed channels of discourse. The crippling limitations of fundamentalist Bible thumpers is hardly more grotesque or less edifying than such conferences as this to which I refer. But here, once again, I am in danger of wandering from my topic. This is a danger that those who are underspecialized are especially vulnerable to; indeed, you do pay a price for everything, especially when you're not aware of it.

Although he was neither a crank nor a bigot, George Peek did have a few quirks. After taking up the ministry, he came to believe that it was wrong for him to wear a tie. This may have been pragmatism sporting an idealistic mask, however; he may have learned to disapprove of ties when he couldn't afford to buy one. But there's no real evidence that this is the case; and I suspect it was not so, or he would have told us. Whatever the cause, his conviction was strong. "Why does the preacher wear a tie anyway?" he asks rhetorically at the beginning of Chapter 21. "They used to say it protected their shirt fronts, when they were accosted [*sic*] in regard to their large cravats. Others thought them too conspicuous and contended [*sic*] for a modest little bow."

Evidently, he was true to his conviction, for a contemporary photo of him with his family shows him without a tie, but wearing a shiny white shirt buttoned at the neck. George and his wife are seated together outside, with their seven mostly grown children standing behind, and with trees and what appears to be a barn in the far background. Four of their five sons pictured are wearing bow ties; the fifth may be tieless, or he may be wearing a conventional tie; the photograph does not show clearly, but my guess is that he is tieless. A contrary chip off the old block, or one son out of five who takes upon himself the principle or prejudice—whichever it might prove to be—of his father.

But isn't it impressive that George did not impose tielessness upon all his sons, and still allowed them to have their pictures taken with him? Given the passionate narrowness of some fundamentalist sects, this fact glows with something like a humane and tolerant liberalism.

❦   Some of you who have been counting the words in my title will have noticed that I have not given hound dogs their due. The nearest I have come is a footnote on bull terriers, and that is obviously not enough.

That men in Appalachia take their dogs seriously is clear to just about everybody who knows anything about that strange and backward culture.[1] The breeding and training of good hunting dogs is an art which, like cockfighting, provides an opportunity for its own sort of skill and sophistication. A good coon hound can sell for many hundreds, perhaps thousands, of dollars, and one who knows dogs can look at one and see more than the rest of us hardly believe possible.

Sometimes these coveted and expensive creatures wander off and are lost—or, worse, stolen. Occasionally, local newspapers run an ad asking for the return of an especially prized dog. Sometimes a photo of the dog will be printed in the paper; and for people who know and love dogs, there is nothing in the least whimsical or peculiar in this—although to cat lovers and other odd sorts, all hound dogs look pretty much alike.

George Peek would understand what I am saying. Early in his book, speaking of his days of boyhood innocence, before he was lost, and long before he was saved, he talks of how he had loved hunting:

My grandfather Henderson gave me a beautiful white and black spotted pup that lived to be 18 years old and made a wonderful coon dog. We went hunting one night, and the dog ran a coon up a large Hemlock tree on which were many limbs from the ground up. We had a small shotgun with us, which I stuck down the back of my coat collar and started up the tree in search of Mr. Coon. It was tall and thick limbed, so I went up and up, searching the limbs as I went,

1. I trust that the context will show that I would also claim that it is rich and vital, as well, and possessed of its own woeful sort of beauty.

until I got away up where it was getting small and beginning to weave back and forth. I saw the coon right on the top twig, looking this way and that way as if fixing to jump. I drew my gun and leveled the barrel on him and fired. He dropped right on me; but, as luck would have it, he was too dead to bite or scratch. He had looked down as I pulled the trigger and I filled his forehead full of shot. He weighed twenty-five pounds.

This is one of the best stories in George Peek's book, and it has nothing to do with sin or salvation, not even if you disapprove of hunting. "Too dead to bite or scratch" is a grand phrase, distinguishable from all lesser degrees of being dead by its reference to the coon's inability to . . . well, bite or scratch.

However, the story's only real defect, as I see it, is the omission of that coon dog's name. I would like to know what it was. If we can take pity on fighting cocks, and if George Peek can refer to that wild nocturnal beast formally as "Mr. Coon," surely we have a right to know what his dog was named . . . especially after he had gone to all the trouble to live eighteen years, which—as the clearly inaccurate formula has it—would be 126 years for a human. Well, maybe we're not as far from our woodland neighbors as our laws and conventions suggest.

On the other hand, I wouldn't hesitate one second in sentencing Bambi to death for stealing a handkerchief. Or maybe a fitter punishment would be turning a good Airedale loose on it. But first, I would name the Airedale—something like "Ned" or "Thackeray" . . . or—if it was a *girl*-dog, as I once heard a Tennessee boy refer to a bitch—"Naomi" or "Harriet."

My reference to Airedales has been waiting all this time, even though it isn't exactly a breed of hound. Nevertheless, they were bred into the bear packs of professional hunters in the Great Smokies many years ago. These pack owners needed a dog with enough fire, guts, quickness, and hardness and strength of jaw to close with bears and corner them. Their big, slow, soft-mouthed bloodhounds were excellent at dry trailing, but were useless for closing with a bear.

So, after much study and deliberation, they decided that the Airedale was the blood needed. Airedales are big terriers—of relatively recent vintage, having first been bred in the second half of the nineteenth century; they were created by Yorkshire sportsmen for strength, courage, quickness, and intelligence. Nobody knows the exact recipe these men employed, but it is known that it required many ingredients, some of them still unknown. It is certain, however, that it called for a great amount of otterhound. So the still-thriving descendents of those first Airedales are both terrier and hound; and, as one who has owned two of them, I can't help adding that the result is an utterly splendid breed of dog.

By now, we have exhausted our title, and you have learned a great deal about matters that you probably knew little about. But then, perhaps you didn't much care about these matters; perhaps you didn't think they *mattered*. Perhaps, alas, you still don't.

Well, these are imponderable issues, and I won't dwell upon them any longer. For the fulfilment of a title—good, bad, or merely denotative— has its own aesthetic integrity; and that, we might affirm, is an end to the matter.

❦ The Bracketing of Time

Travel is mysterious because of the triumph of immediacy over memory. Two or three days after we have settled into a hotel or fishing lodge, all about us seems homelike, whereas the images of those places where we have lived for years begin to bleed light and acquire an anaemic transparency. How little time is required for us to "feel at home"; and how perfidious we are in forgetting the dwellings where we have lived so long. We are constantly overwhelmed by immediacy. "The instant my guests leave," Emerson wrote in his journal, "they show as ghosts."

Emerson's testimony refers to something intrinsic in the way we process time. The density of a present reality bullies our senses into a numb forgetfulness of past truths. I think the universality of this impression may have only one exception, but that is the greatest of all. I speak of time itself.

Time is the one place where we have all come to visit. I am aware there is deceit in this metaphor, for who *was* there to travel before we got here? Still, this figure has its pointedness, and in the present context will prove useful. If we go to Mackinack Island and settle in comfortably, it will soon become the only reality we can feel. Those other, more abstract, realities of past events and places will require some effort for us to visualize clearly, just as the thought of Mackinack Island is remote to us now (if we are not presently there), and the clopping of horse hooves on the cobblestones only an enchanting notion of an island that has been deliberately put aside. "Out of time," as we say.

And yet, time itself does not afford such perspectives. Precisely as we live, we experience time. We do this even when we seem, momentarily, to step outside, to enter another "time frame," wherein we experience time microcosmically, in another matrix. We say this when we become absorbed in a good book or are beguiled by the powerfully rendered "reality" of a good show on television or at the theater.

But these are serifs upon the lettering of time, and time itself does not casually lend itself to metaphorical reconstruction. We are inserted into time, and then we are removed—as the dates on chronological charts of the famous dead so clearly indicate. During my decades of active booking I have always bought "chronologies" when I have come upon them; but after buying them, I've never quite known what to do with them. They cannot be read as texts; and yet, like those other, more common maps, they are delightful to contemplate and study.

Not all chronologies are organized on this lateral principle. Years ago, I bought THE OXFORD CHRONOLOGICAL TABLE OF ANCIENT HISTORY, SYNCHRONISTICALLY AND ETHNOGRAPHICALLY ARRANGED, Oxford, 1838—bound together with its "modern" sequel, published in 1840. Responsive to the raggedness of human events, it features vertical bands on both pages, chronologically progressive from top to bottom. These bands are cultural as well as geographical, and one can follow synchronous events from left to right across both pages, covering a rich variety of subjects, including Saxons, Franks, and Goths (p. 23) along with Physics, Architecture, Music, and "Luxury, Manners, and Customs" (p. 37, where we are given such bulletins as: "In A.D. 41, Women possess great influence at the imperial court under Claudius," and in 218, "Heliogabalus [was] the most debauched of the emperors—he was the first who wore silk, which after him came into general vogue."

There is something both majestic and futile about human attempts to devise maps for time, or at least temporal human events; and most of us respond to the adventure and ambition in such enterprise. But the OXFORD CHRONOLOGY just referred to is not precisely what is required as a model for what follows; I am thinking of that more common sort of chronology which plots historical events laterally under dates that proceed from left to right, chronologically, across the page. These dates place "in time" the accomplishments of great historical figures somewhere in the white spaces between their births and deaths, thereby inviting us to see purely temporal connections that are always instructive, and often surprising.

These birth and death dates are indicated by brackets that enclose what might be thought of as the temporal visits of famous people. Looking at these bracketed time-spans, we see that the lives of Benjamin Franklin and Samuel Johnson overlapped significantly, as did those of Mark Twain and Tolstoy; while those of Stephen Crane and Hemingway overlapped just barely (Hemingway was born in 1897 and Crane died in 1900).

The brackets on chronological charts also mark "what sorts of time" people have lived in. Constantly we acknowledge the uniquenesses of generations. We say, "It was a time when such things happened," and know what we mean. But underneath every *Zeitgeist* there is the fact of change, which is both the manifestation and instrument of time. No matter what different sorts of symbolic clocks are built into a language or culture, the fact of time is somehow represented, and it necessarily allows for substantive change. But in spite of this universality, and in contrast to a vacation on Mackinack Island, time does not become more familiar to us "in time," though it may become increasingly taken-for-granted; it becomes stranger. Time is a place where, the longer you visit there, the stranger it seems.

This is my subject; and I think there is none more majestic, more perplexing, and more interesting. Part of the problem has to do with the different varieties of time, the different masks it wears. We assume that the same ontological clock is ticking away beneath all of our impressions; and yet, it is hard for us to believe that the five minutes spent waiting for the announcement of the winner in the third race is the same five minutes spent sleeping. Or perhaps reading from Emerson's journals.

All of these times are going on all the time in our bodies and heads; and also, with different phasing and at different rates, they are going on with others. I do not for a moment assume that one of my fifty minute classes has the same duration for my students as it does for me; nor do I assume that it is equal among them. Unannounced examinations covering the "material covered" will be one indication of this diversity of times.

The bracketing of dates on chronological charts shows what a great reach we possess as speaking, literate, historically minded creatures, and what dramatic linkages and overlaps can be seen in our time spans. I am not very elderly as measured by today's clocks in the Western World, but I was four years old when Wyatt Earp died in 1929. Given the occasion,

I would have been old enough to hear him tell stories of his experiences in the old west, although I would not have understood very much, because what could this old man have had to say to a four-year old boy?

At about that age I did , however, meet Ken Maynard—perhaps, next to Tom Mix, the most famous cowboy star of early films—when he was visiting his relatives, who were also friends of my parents, in Upper Arlington, a Columbus, Ohio, suburb. For all I know, Ken Maynard may have played the part of Wyatt Earp in one of his many films; but I can't remember that he did, nor can I remember anything he said, although he picked me up and let me sit on his knee.

To return to Wyatt Earp, the real western hero, in contrast to the film version, the overlap in our dates strikes me as wonderful—think of it, during those four years the legendary frontier law officer and I shared "the same time," which seems mysteriously edifying, in some way, although I'm not certain what way this might be.

But the overlap of human lifespans can be far more impressive than this. Within the past decade, as this is written, I met an old man who claimed to be the only living person who could remember talking with a survivor of the New Madrid earthquake. This was that cosmic convulsion throughout the midwest that changed the course of the Mississippi River and created Reelfoot Lake. Written records show that the earth shook for a Biblical forty days and forty nights, and it is no wonder that people gathered together to pray and sing hymns. Nor is it any wonder that, after the earth stopped jumping, they should peek out, reconsider, and set forth to take up their lives pretty much where they had left off.

And, soon, time would have established all the old comfortably secure and predictable boredoms, as surely as if the earthquake had left everybody in some vacation land of safety, forgetful of that violence that had been their home for forty days. Maybe we would all be wiser if the earth shook us up periodically to let us know that being able to stand still and look at a motionless sycamore tree is a subtle miracle.

The old gentleman who could remember talking with a survivor of the New Madrid earthquake was named Quint Guier, and he was the father of Martha Guier, the director of the Jesse Stuart Writers' Conference, in Murray, Kentucky, where I taught the course in novel writing one summer in the late 1970's. Mr. Guier was a "student" in one of the conference classes. The year of the New Madrid earthquake? 1811 and 1812—a time when Jefferson was living at Monticello, Emerson was still a schoolboy, and Franz Joseph Haydn had been dead for only two years.

Quint Guier's life and mine overlapped for a brief period (almost certainly he is dead now), and he told me what he had heard about that almost unbelievably distant time. It was his great great grandmother, as I remember, who had told him about the earthquake. Mr. Guier, I should state, was a perfectly lucid and rational man—even though he was halfway through his tenth decade when he told me the stories he'd heard about how all the people had gathered together in certain places and prayed and sang hymns, expecting the end of the world at any moment. The earthquake itself would have been enough to turn one's mind toward apocalyptic matters; but everything was rendered even more dramatic because of recent dire predictions from the clergy that Armageddon was fast approaching. The earthquake must have struck all churchgoers, and many infidels, as the climax to the worldly drama. And when it ended, with the world still pretty much intact, the survivors had to learn to live with the fact and accept the anti-climax against all theological, or at least pastoral, prompting.

❧   In 1970, almost a decade before I met Mr. Guier, I learned that there were at that time three "Indian scouts" still receiving government pensions. I was spending the year as Writer in Residence at Wichita State University, and decided that I wanted mightily to interview one or more of those survivors from a mythic past.

To get the names and addresses of these men, I wrote to the government pension office, explaining what I had in mind. My request was subjected to what I would suppose is a more-or-less typical bureaucratic interpretation, which is to say, I received a prompt reply stating that the names and addresses of pensioners were not revealed in order to "protect them from solicitation." I marvelled over this answer. Did some functionary in Washington really suppose I was going to approach one of these old fellows and try to sell him a motorcycle or life insurance policy?

Fortunately, I had a friend in The U.S. House of Representatives who

knew me well enough to swear that I couldn't sell life insurance to a rich
man on the sinking Titanic. This was Clarence Brown, from Urbana,
Ohio—an old-time neighbor—who, in the way of good neighbors and
representatives, gave prompt and ungrudging assistance, so that I soon
had the names and addresses of all three of these old scouts.

I remember that one of the survivors lived in Chicago and another in
Mill Valley, California. I cannot remember where the third lived, because
I didn't receive an answer to my inquiry about him, and his place of
residence is forgotten. But I remember the other two, because I received
answers from women who were taking care of them. One of these old men
was said to be in a terminal coma, and the other was so senile that he
could not be depended on to give a clear answer to any conceivable sort
of question.

So I was too late, and that was pretty much that. But the frustration of
this particular plan reminded me of a far-more reprehensible failure a
quarter of a century before that. While serving as a radioman on a Coast
Guard cutter out of Sitka, Alaska, I decided to get a part-time job.
We were out on anti-submarine patrol one week, then in port the next,
alternating with the Aurora, another of similar size and class.

I asked around and was told that there were openings for orderlies in
the old Alaskan Pioneers Home in Sitka. I didn't know anything about
this place, or exactly what my duties would be; but it didn't sound very
interesting, so I forgot about it. I supposed that I would naturally be given
menial tasks, cleaning up the rooms and giving baths to old men and
maybe pushing them around in wheel chairs. What else was I trained to
do?

It wasn't until some years later that I realized what an opportunity I had
rejected. Unquestionably, many of these old Alaskan pioneers had been
part of the gold rush of the 1890's. Think of the stories I might have
heard! Some of them might have known the inspiration for the legendary
Dangerous Dan McGrew, or maybe even that real Irishman, Mike Malo-
ney, who all by himself carried a piano over the Chilkoot Pass on a trail
that was said to be so steep some men could not even climb it unburdened.

But none of this was to be. I should have known better, for I lived in a
time when the cult of experience flourished and it was fashionable for a
young, apprentice writer to go out into the world and do and see things

so that he would have "something to write about." And what experiences could have been more interesting than the stories these old men might have told, if I had been able to listen well?

There is much that is hypothetical in this, of course; but that doesn't inhibit the memory and the vagueness of a sort of guilt focusing upon a sin of omission that must always have a special significance for a writer. And this guilt has a most specific form: what rich material there must have been for me to gather!

❦   All of this brings us by a curious route to my father's law offices, many years ago located on the eighth floor of the Outlook Building, at 44 East Broad Street, in Columbus. His office was directly across from the Ohio Capitol; and often when there was a parade, we would gather there and watch from above. I clearly remember the Armistice Day parades, led by a marching band, then followed by a dozen or so old men dressed in black or dark blue suits. Only a few wore their old uniforms, with campaign ribbons and medals pinned to their jackets. Some had long white whiskers—an odd sight in those days—and a few were painfully bent over, leaning on canes as they prodded their slow progress in the vanguard.

These were the Civil War veterans, of course, followed in turn by Spanish American War Veterans, and then the great mass of those from World War I, striding straight and tall, many in their old khaki uniforms. I remember watching one of these parades—it may have been the last I watched—when there were only two or three of the "boys in blue" left to lead the host of veterans past the Outlook Building—probably just barely able to hear the music played by the band ahead. As I remember it, the Civil War did not seem so distant to me then as it does now. Of course, literally it was not. But I am not speaking of that; I am speaking of the time required to render a period mythic in the imagination, so that the instant the last Civil War veteran died, there was a slippage in human history, one access to a fabled time lost forever.

The Outlook Building from which we watched was a handsome and interesting landmark of that time. There were elevators run by levers manipulated by "elevator boys" who wore uniforms and small military-style caps. Barnes' drugstore was on the first floor. Like the building's lobby, it had a marble floor, a stained carved wooden counter, and wire-backed chairs that were functional and modern then, but are today much admired for their quaintness. I drank my first chocolate milkshake in Barnes' drugstore, and I can also remember many times ordering "a lime phosphate without the phosphate"—which seemed to me a curious formula then, as it does even today; and I have no clear idea of what it actually was. But that was the correct formula for ordering it, and it tasted good.

In the basement of this building, there was a great, resonant Men's Room, with a black man as attendant, a "shoe-shine boy". The walls and floors were solid marble, and it was probably a great place to whistle. I suspect I often took advantage of the acoustics, for I was fortunate in my boyhood—spoiled, no doubt, and certainly uninhibited. But whistling in one's boyhood is hardly possessed of that emphasis necessary for remembering, unless it evokes some striking response . . . as when, at the age of five, I started to climb Lincoln's seated statue in the Lincoln Memorial in Washington, and a policeman tapped me with his club, motioning for me to climb back down. I was mightily embarrassed, and remember that incident well, along with the amusement of my parents, who evidently found nothing at all alarming in the episode.

But to return to the Outlook Building: not too far away from the Men's Room in the basement, there was a large barber shop (marble, again: marble was everywhere), with perhaps a half-dozen barber chairs, and friendly and attentive barbers, along with a manicurist who had her own table and chairs in the corner. These women came and went, and I cannot remember what any of them looked like, exactly; but I have a general impression that they were all very attractive, perfumed, and vividly "made-up." Perhaps there was a slight taint of harlotry in their lavish use of cosmetics—relative to the ways of that time, of course. Probably I imagined it, but they always seemed especially pleased to see me. There weren't many young boys who frequented the Outlook Building. These women made over me, and asked such uninteresting questions as "how I liked school." (I was not supposed to like it very much, and of course understood this fact.) Now, all these years later, I sometimes wonder what their solicitous smiling cost them, for no great perceptiveness is needed to realize that smiling was an essential part of their charm, which was essential to their livelihood. But at the time, I was incapable of seeing the dark other side of appearances, and accepted their friendliness as only natural. No doubt men as well as women had their nails polished by these women, but my father was never among them—nor can I imagine his ever being so.

In my father's law firm there were eight lawyers, plus several secretaries—one of whom, Miss Alkire, was with him as long as I can remember. She was a slender, well-groomed, quiet-voiced woman of great efficiency and calm. And yet it seemed to me that there was always a strained expression on her pale, powdered face. In my memory, her appearance was strikingly like that of my home room teacher at Crestview Junior High School, in Clintonville, a suburb of north Columbus. My home room teacher was also thin, and very tense, and she hardly talked above a whisper. I think I was a special trial to her, although I can't remember exactly why. But I can remember her often whispering at me out of a nervous expression, so I have to assume that I often misbehaved. Nevertheless, I don't think I ever disliked this poor woman, and I hope that somehow she realized this, because I have a strong impression that I was something of a problem and that she worried about me a great deal. She seemed to spend a lot of time watching me. It was said that her face was so heavily powdered because it had been badly burned at one time; but certainly, I can't remember that she was disfigured in any way. I remember her as a kind and very conscientious woman, and I will never forget her wonderful name, Hedwig Bretz.

But to return to my father's secretary: the last time I specifically remember seeing Miss Alkire was one frigid, snowy winter's night after I'd come home from the service in World War II. My father, in poor health, had worked late this evening, keeping Miss Alkire overtime to finish some business at hand. For different reasons, my sister and I were downtown, and we met at our father's office, so that I could drive—for the streets were very icy. We drove Miss Alkire to her apartment near the university. I enjoyed driving my father's new 1946 Buick, with my sister and him sitting in back. Miss Alkire sat in front and complimented me on my driving, saying that it was the first time she had ridden in a car on such an icy surface and not been nervous.

I still think of Miss Alkire, and wonder if her life was as lonely as it seems to me now. As lonely, say, as that of Hedwig Bretz. And of course I remember Miss Alkire's compliment, for compliments—like the tap of a policeman's club when you are five years old—are likely to have great staying power in the memory.

I often think of the Outlook Building at 44 East Broad Street, directly facing the Ohio Capitol, which we could look down upon from the Olympian perspective afforded by my father's office. The Outlook Building was handsome, in its way; but now it is entirely gone, replaced by a building that is vastly larger in every way, and which would be entirely alien and anonymous to me if I were to step inside. But I was "there," in that place, before those who now inhabit the new building could have recognized it. And if in some mysterious way I could walk into the lobby of the old Outlook Building, I am sure it would all seem entirely familiar. Barnes' drugstore would be to the right as I enter, and the elevator operators would be standing ahead of me in their clean, neat uniforms, looking friendly, waiting to take me up to the eighth floor.

❦   I don't know when the Outlook Building was erected, nor do I know exactly when it was torn down to make room for the much larger, more modern, more efficient office building that has taken its place, along with the places of the old buildings on both sides, whose names I cannot remember. But this building was inserted into history at one time and taken out in another, just as all temporal things are. It was one temporal thing, and I am another, and our times overlapped for twenty years or so. Our histories are linked together during this time, and it was part of the reality that I grew up in—a building, a place, that was much like many others in the 1930's, but would today seem quaint and old-fashioned. A few old resort hotels, it seems to me, retain certain features of that time and place; but there can't be many, and the few that remain are not likely to be around much longer.

In my father's view, the Outlook Building must have seemed the essence of modernity. For example, virtually all elevators at that time were manually operated by a man or woman, who used a brass lever that opened and closed the humming electrical circuits; these had to be lifted and dropped at just the right time for the elevator to glide to floor level. Often, another nudge or two, up or down, was required to get it exactly level. "Watch your step, please," they would say as you got off, for some small variance in the levels was inevitable.

The first escalator I ever saw was in a department store in Toronto in 1937, and it seemed a marvel of technology. Think of it: *a gliding stairway!* It wasn't long after this that escalators were installed everywhere, and virtually all elevators became passenger-operated, automatically taking one to the designated floor, with no nudges required and requiring no more skill than being able to read numerals and press a button. Getting off, you hardly had to watch your step, for accurate alignment was a built-in feature.

My father lived to see these new marvels, but they were not of his natural time. Our natural time is the period when our sense of the world is formed; so that even today, when I encounter the word "restaurant," the image evoked is that of a store-front building with big plate windows and cars parked parallel on the street in front. This is a pre-1950 version, and of course my father's image of "restaurant" must have been far older than that.

He was born on November 15, 1890, when Herman Melville and Walt Whitman were still living. And he was alive when the Battle of Wounded Knee was fought. Such bracketing is meaningful, even though that meaning is limited to an abstract and theoretical temporal intersection, since he was less than two months old when that dismal business happened. But it is a fact, and a rather strange one to contemplate, that he was born into a world which was verging upon an unnecessary and horrible calamity that would take place a thousand miles away some fifty-nine days later.

Years afterwards, however, my father experienced a much more tangible and mythic connection with the Old West. One day when he was driving his car, an old Model T, over the muddy roads in Gallia County in southern Ohio, he came upon an old man walking in the same direction and stopped and offered him a ride, which was accepted.

His passenger was poorly dressed and missing one of his eyes. He was old and wrinkled, with very dark weathered skin. My father asked about him, as was the habit in those days, and was told a very strange story. The old man said that he had lost his eye at the Battle of the Little Big Horn.

He said he had been one of Custer's Indian scouts, and having had his eye shot out and being covered with blood, hid himself among the corpses so he wouldn't be killed. Then, after nightfall, he crept away and made his escape. I don't recall any explanation of why he wasn't scalped. Perhaps he had been, and was wearing a hat which concealed the fact, when my father gave him a ride.

This was all that I remember hearing about the episode; but I do remember that as a small boy I wanted mightily to believe every word of it. What a magic connection this would have been if it had been true! Now, so many years later, I find the magic there anyway, no matter what the truth of the story may have been.

For to me, this was a great adventure whether the old Indian told the story from memory, or simply made up a colorful lie. The bracketing of time allowed for the possibility of his story being true, whether it was or not—and now it would be impossible for anybody to find out the truth, anyway. And the simple fact that this old man, like some cousin of the ancient mariner, had an epic story to tell—one that *might conceivably have been true*—conveys its own sort of magic, since as a species we always hunger for stories, and always will. "Man creates legends," Edward Dahlberg wrote, "so that he will not have a mean existence."

❦ Several years ago, I heard of an elderly man in Middleport, Ohio, on the Ohio River, who was supposed to have some letters written by Mark Twain. His name was Rodney Downing, and when I phoned him, I learned that he had indeed *once* possessed some of Mark Twain's letters, but they'd all been lost in the 1913 flood.

"All of them?" I asked.

Yes, he was pretty sure they'd all been lost. But there seemed to be the faintest whiff of doubt in the old gentleman's voice, so when he kindly invited me to come visit him sometime, I accepted. Thus it was that before long I was chatting with Mr. Downing, and learned that his great grandfather, "Captain Jack" Downing, had been mentioned in Twain's *Life on the Mississippi.* In fact, the old man had known Sam Clemens when he was on the river, and told stories about him. He was the one to whom Twain had written the letters.

"What sorts of stories?" I asked.

Well, that was a long time ago. But one of them had to do with the helmsman crying out that they'd either just hit a sandbar or else they'd run over some alligators. This had the right tone to it, and I looked it up in *Life on the Mississippi*, where it was reported somewhat as Rodney Downing told it, although with considerably more detail and outrageous exaggeration.

The scene takes place up in the pilot house, where the pilot is sharing river lore with the young Mark Twain, and casually refers to an odd-looking vessel passing by as an "alligator boat."

"An alligator boat? What's it for?"

"To dredge out alligators with."

"Are they so thick as to be troublesome?"

"Well, not now, because the government keeps them down. But they used to be. Not everywhere; but in favorite places, here and there, where the river is wide and shoal—like Plum Point, and Stack Island, and so on—places they call alligator beds."

This goes on for a while, and then the pilot mentions how hard it used to be to identify alligator water:

"Of course there were some few pilots that could judge of alligator water nearly as well as they could of any other kind, but they had to have natural talent for it; it wasn't a thing a body could *learn*, you had to be born with it. Let me see: there was Ben Thornburg, and Beck Jolly, and Squire Bell, and Horace Bixby, and Major Downing, and John Stevenson, and Billy Gordon, and Jim Brady, and George Ealer, and Billy Youngblood—all A 1 alligator pilots. *They* could tell alligator water as far as another Christian could tell whiskey. Read it?—Ah, *couldn't* they, though! I only wish I had as many dollars as they could read alligator water a mile and a half off.[1]

1. *Life on the Mississippi*, Bost., 1883. pp. 266–7.

This is pure, 100 proof, vintage Mark Twain, even to promoting Captain Jack Downing to Major, and listing names—which is an act of creation dear to the writer's heart, even if they are real names . . . and, last but not least, muddling a perfectly promising metaphor at the end so that it squeaks like a bad axle.

Or was Rodney Downing's version of his grandfather's nickname mistaken? Possibly. I didn't raise the question, of course, but later I couldn't help but wonder—had old Mr. Downing's version come from his grandfather's reminiscences, or from the book itself? The two versions are obviously related, but of course they might both have been variations upon an old river joke, and not a stupendously funny one at that when translated out of Twain's idiom.

During my visit with Mr. Downing, however, I was reluctant to dwell too long upon such questions. I asked him in several ways if some of the letters might not have survived. I pointed out that things like letters get put in odd places and pop up when you least expect them. Like alligators, in a way.

But it just didn't work. In spite of my persistence, Rodney Downing was not able to think of anyplace where the letters might be. He was almost certain they had been lost in the flood, and eventually I was constrained to believe him. Nevertheless, in view of the fact that he was such a courteous and interesting old gentleman, I did not regret having travelled to Middleport. Here was a natural story teller, and sometimes when your mind is intent upon one thing (i.e., buying old letters or books), you can listen to a man like this talk for half an hour before you come awake to the fact that the talk itself is worth hearing, independent of its leading to the achievement of some extraneous goal (acquiring letters and/or books) you've had in mind.

Mr. Downing's reminiscences were technically of the second-hand variety, for they were stories he'd heard old men tell when he was a boy. But he had a way of talking, and that's what matters, after all. He told several stories he'd heard from old soldiers about the Civil War. He mentioned a local boy who'd joined the Union Army and had been on board a gunboat when it had floated down past Memphis, and a squad of Union soldiers—mistaking it for a Rebel boat—had opened fire on it. Years after the event, two of the local Civil War veterans in Middleport were talking about their adventures in the army, and when the one mentioned this incident where the boat had been fired upon by her own men, another one yelled out in surprise: "Were *you* on that boat? Why, I was one of the boys that was standing there shooting at you!" And the two of them got a great laugh out of it, having survived the incident and looking back upon it from the vantage point of fifty or sixty years.

Rodney Downing talked about his great grandfather, who as an old man liked to sit in a chair and have little Rodney comb his long white hair. The Downings were an old river family, the first to migrate (from Maine)—that first one, also named Rodney, coming down the Ohio River and raising his family there. Stillman Larkin in *The Pioneer History of Meigs County*, wrote that "Rodney Downing built a steamboat, the Gen. Harrison, at the Stedman farm on Leading creek, in 1835, intended for the Cincinnati and New Orleans trade."[1] (I like the thought of a time so distant that a steamboat could be built on somebody's *farm!*)

John B. Downing must have been a great old alligator pilot for Twain to write letters to him after so much time and fame had come between them, and no doubt he had plenty of his own stories to tell. After all, as Twain made clear, not just anybody could become an alligator pilot back in those days.

Then Rodney told another story about one of the local veterans, and how he'd made his way back home after the war. I can't remember either the details or the substance of this story, or what point there was to it—except for the fact that this old gentleman was a good-enough story teller to make it all seem pleasant and worthwhile at the time.

But near the end of this particular yarn, Rodney Downing did something extraordinary. He mentioned that the soldier had made his way back home through Clarksburg, West Virginia—but when he said this, *he turned and pointed upriver!*

How different our shared realities are! For Rodney Downing, the old soldier's homecoming was a fact that existed in a place he knew and felt

1. Cols., Ohio, 1908. Larkin also refers to "Major Downing" rather than "Captain," which would seem to corroborate Twain's reference; but of course, Larkin himself may have gotten the reference from Twain, even though Larkin was a "local boy" and should have known first hand.

next to him. It was *Clarksburg* that soldier had marched through over a century before, and that Clarksburg still lay a hundred and fifty or so miles to the east in this old gentleman's imagination. The Civil War was revealed, in that simple gesture, as existing for Rodney Downing in a way that it could not exist for me, because, for me—in spite of my dim memories of seeing veterans of Shiloh and Chickamauga marching west on Broad Street in Columbus on Armistice Day . . . for me, that war is mythic and distant, a place that exists solely in the imagination as evoked by pictures and print. But for Rodney Downing, part of it still existed as something he could *point to*, as told to him when he was a small boy by an old veteran; and the Clarksburg that this soldier boy had travelled through all those years before was still there, upriver and inland—as tangible and real, if not as reachable, as Parkersburg or Marietta.

❦ Something of this innate tenacity to retain old things is essential to the coherence we need for the events that comprise our lives to connect with one another and "add up." I can understand this well, and often think of it. And there are times when such thoughts are far from mere whimsical self-indulgence or the mind-rub of nostalgia.

Still, for example, whenever I am in Columbus and have occasion to travel east on Broad Street from High, I pass the Capitol building on my right—a familiar and splendid old monstrosity that has never had its dome completed after standing there for almost one hundred and fifty years. I pass this, and then glance to my left, where I can so well remember the Outlook Building standing. The unnamed building that has replaced it is a vast and overwhelming presence; but for part of me, it is only a mockery of something that I once knew to have been true and real.

A Note about the Author

Jack Matthews is a novelist, essayist, poet, short story writer, and Distinguished Professor of English at Ohio University, in Athens, where he and his wife live and deal in old and rare books.